Praise for IT WENT

MW00633095

What a privilege to be allowed into a family and learn the raw lessons their experiences have to teach all of us. John, Joyce and Jamie are completely real and open. Their journey touches you in a way that is both emotional and inspiring. *It Went Without Saying* draws you in and keeps you absorbed to the end. It did me.

—Bobbi DePorter, President, Quantum Learning Network/SuperCamp
Author, *Quantum Success*

It Went Without Saying offers an intimate insight into the profound shame and low self-esteem that often accompany learning disabilities and mental-health problems. As the story unfolded, my heart went out to the young child who believed that something was wrong with her. I couldn't put the book down as I experienced how, in an attempt to ease the pain associated with her learning disabilities, the child became an addict. By sharing their story, this brave family will help countless others know they are not alone.

—Diane Woodward, MSW, Developmental Disability Consultant

Within the pages of this book, I have found the words. Within the words, I have found an antidote to the pain, fear, isolation and degradation of this insidious disease. I'm reminded once again that it is truth that will set you free. The journey this family traveled to find the truth was paved with all of the barriers and life-threatening hardships so well known to the addict and the family, and so unknown to those spared by the disease. This is a beautiful story of triumph, manifested by the perception of defeat. It is the story of spiritual beings conquering a very real and dangerous human condition, through love and hope.

—Kevin Rosell, CIT, RSAT-PA, Addictions Counselor

It Went Without Saying is courageous and powerful. The Chupkas have opened their hearts, shared their deepest-held secrets and, by taking us through their own process, have created an opening for healing for other families impacted by addiction. Their willingness to dig deep, to expose their flaws, their mistakes and their discoveries throughout this journey, is a beacon for others who are struggling with the same issues they avoided, denied and ultimately had the courage to face. My lifework has been devoted to the treatment of addiction and I have experienced the devastating toll it takes on individuals and families. This book is a vitally important voice for all of us. I am deeply grateful for them and for this groundbreaking work.

—Dr. Cheryl L. Clark, Director, Shock Incarceration,
New York State Department of Correctional Services,
author of *DOING LIFE! A Life-Skills Program for Recovery from Addiction*
and *S.M.A.R.T. Choices! A Life-Skills Program for Making Choices That Work*

It may have gone without saying, but this book says it all—at least for me as the parent of an addict and alcoholic. It was a page-turner that I wish I could have read when my son was still in high school. The disease is powerful, waiting for my child to be most vulnerable, waiting in the wings to consume him. My hope is that he will know that life is good and will choose sobriety. Thank you for giving me hope.

—Mother of an active alcoholic/addict

IT WENT WITHOUT SAYING

. . . .

A Family's Journey from Addiction to Recovery

JOHN, JOYCE AND JAMIE CHUPKA

To order additional copies of this title, contact your favorite local bookstore or visit www.itwentwithoutsaying.com

Book and cover design by Anne C. Smith, The Troy Book Makers.

Printed in the United States of America

The Troy Book Makers
www.thetroybookmakers.com

ISBN: 978-1-935534-372

THIS BOOK IS DEDICATED TO

· · · · ·

Hannah Rose Chupka,
who fills our home with life, love and boundless energy.

• •

MAY ALL WHOSE EYES *make contact with ours through the pages of this book become less burdened. May the shame and judgment attached to addiction be transformed by a compassionate heart. May we walk hand in hand to reclaim our innocence. May we create a future where tolerance and appreciation of differences prevail. Let us do this together, one moment at a time.*

Contents

Prologue

JAMIE TOOK HER first drink a few weeks after she turned 14. By the time she was 18, she was a full-blown alcoholic. Booze was always the baseline, but when she was introduced to coke, her addiction threatened her very existence.

Over the 16 years from the time she took her first drink, Jamie descended into the consuming hell of addiction. There she encountered broken promises, broken bones, blackouts, a violent rape, driving-while-intoxicated (DWI) arrests, hospitalizations, broken hearts and a shattered life.

At 30, after multiple attempts, Jamie finally got clean. She graduated from college. She became a mother. Now she is an addiction counselor. She speaks to diverse audiences about the impact addiction has on families and communities.

The price Jamie paid for her highs was exorbitant, parts of it almost unspeakable. It's not a pretty story.

But here's the thing: Jamie isn't the only one who lost almost 20 years to addiction. She isn't the only one who suffered, deeply, painfully, horribly. She isn't the only one who is in recovery. There were others involved. Her parents suffered with her every step of the way.

This is a story told in the voices of a family of three sober adults who have been through hell and back. This discussion could not have taken place during the years Jamie was lost. Addiction has a way of shutting down every meaningful attempt at real connections. It has a way of isolating people in their pain. It has a way of amplifying the fears of the people involved. It whispers the threat of what can happen if the secret is revealed.

The family has decided to expose the secret and share this story because it offers a new perspective. The reader will enter the web of denial and experience the pain, the fear, the love, the confusion and the desperation with the mother, father and daughter from each of their perspectives.

It is a story that may be similar to your story or that of someone you know. It was written so that people who are grappling with addiction will hear a message that inspires, encourages and offers an antidote to fear.

. . . .

ONE

The Beast Is Real

JOYCE: On the day Jamie was born, I promised her I would protect her from the evils of the world. I would be her shield from harm. What I came to realize was that I could never protect her from the demons she created in her mind—the demons that became real and almost consumed her.

When Jamie was ten, she became enthralled with the movie *Poltergeist*, a horror movie about a beast who took a little girl, Carol Ann, from her living room while she watched TV. Jamie loved that movie. She watched it over and over. She was particularly taken by the strange little psychic who helped the parents rescue their daughter from the beast. The woman had a voice so peculiar that one had to strain to understand what she was saying. Jamie could do a perfect imitation of that voice and she loved to tease me by mimicking one of the psychic's speeches.

She would say, "I don't know whatever's over this house, but it's strong enough to punch a hole in this world and take your daughter away from you. It keeps Carol Ann close to it and away from the spectral light. It lies to her, it tells her things only a child would understand.

It has been using her to restrain the others. To her, it is simply another child. To us, it is the beast."

"Stop, Jamie," I'd say. "It's horrible and scary." But it was a little prank she loved to play. And we could laugh and dismiss it because, after all, it was just a movie. It wasn't real. But something extremely powerful and terrifying really did reach into our lives and take our daughter away from us. And there was no way to dismiss it. When Jamie was 14, a beast took hold of her life—and it was real, very, very real.

The Beast had a name. Its name was Addiction.

As I look at Jamie now, I can hardly believe how close The Beast came to taking her forever, how it almost destroyed her. It is painful to acknowledge how she lied and stole and cheated and hurt everyone around her. Mostly, it's painful to remember how often she hurt herself while we tried in vain to save her. And while it's almost unbearable to reveal this, I must admit that at the end, we started to plan her funeral.

I always believed that love was powerful enough to cure anything. I thought that if you loved someone with all your heart, that love would be reason enough to want to live. I deeply believed my love was strong enough to keep my daughter alive. But I was wrong. The Beast that was consuming her didn't respond to that love. In fact, it was repelled by our love, as a vampire is repelled by light. At the height of Jamie's struggle with The Beast, she told us our love was killing her. The more we told her how much we cared for her, the louder The Beast spoke to her of unworthiness.

So we came to the point of surrender. The strongest tool I knew seemed to have no power at all. I finally realized that if I really believed in unconditional love, I would have to surrender to it. I would have to surrender to what I understood to be God's will. I had to find the strength to believe that our love is only a shadow of a more perfect love. I had to trust that she would be loved in ways I could not imagine. It didn't come easily, but I finally began to accept the fact that my love wasn't keeping her alive. I finally understood that only she and God could decide her destiny. The only choice I had to make was how I would walk through her choice with love in my heart.

Over time, I came to know that I was just as powerless as Jamie was over her addiction. It was *not* something I wanted to admit, but I had to. When I took the first step and admitted I had no power to save her, Jamie was free to decide for herself if she would live.

For all those years, I thought my actions, my will and my dedication to her were keeping her alive. I thought it was my intention for her to be well that was giving her life. Now I know it wasn't. It was a higher power.

JOHN: I never dreamed it could happen again. I thought it had already occurred and I was free of it—like having the measles and not having to worry about getting them again because you've already had them. That is why I was so surprised when it took over our lives. When it did, I did not want to know.

I had already been through the ravages of alcohol and its impact on the lives of a family. I wanted to avoid a replay of that scenario and somehow create this fantasy of a family that I had wished I had when I was young. I was determined to have that family, despite the experiences that were indicating that something was amiss.

I find my childhood experience of alcohol difficult to describe. I know I hated it. It always got in the way. It overpowered me and particularly my father. It came between us without ever saying a word. I resented the way he greeted the Melrose Whiskey when he walked in the door after a hard day's work. I yearned for him to pick me up or stoop down to me and hold me in his arms the way his hands cupped the shot glass as the whiskey seemed to please his senses. I ached for him to look into my eyes and say, "Let's play some ball" or "Let's just sit together for a while." I became jealous of the potion that seemed to ease him. It seemed to give him something that I could not. That was the beginning of "I am not enough." I carried that sadness with me for a very long time.

When alcohol revisited my home during Jamie's adolescence, one might think I would have recognized it early and put an end to it by saying, "Not on my watch and not in my house." I didn't. It played itself out in a similar pattern.

I was unprepared to meet the challenge. Ever since I was young, I had watched how my mother coped with this intruder. She made excuses, minimized its damage, found the good in the man and remained afraid to confront the situation. Unbeknownst to me, my mind was already encoding a road map of how to deal with this situation if and when it was to occur in my life.

When the unwanted guest appeared at our doorstep, my mind automatically went to that imprinted mental road map. The important thing to know is that my mind did not think about how to close the door on this guest. It went to how to deal with the guest while it was in my house. It went downhill fast from there.

It got so bad at the end of Jamie's using that we forced ourselves to face the possibility that she could die. I remember being terrified of the phone's ringing late at night, because I was sure that it would be the call telling us she was dead. As with Joyce, I knew that we had to let go. I had to let go of the things I wanted for her, my hopes and dreams for her life. Most important, I had to let go of my fears. I was so afraid of life without her. I didn't want to live with the relentless judgment I would place on myself for her death. I told myself that if I could let go of that terror, I just might be able to have a moment of peace. From that peace I could build another moment of peace.

Something Was Not Quite Right

JAMIE: I was born in love. I was brought up with love. I was surrounded by love. My parents, my parents' friends—everyone loved me. I was loved enough for three people. From the outside looking in, there was nothing wrong. I had a really great life. But from the inside looking out, there was always something wrong. There was always something missing in me—something that wasn't quite right. Something was telling me I wasn't okay, that I was different. From a very early age, I didn't like who I was, and I remember it so clearly. I was an only child, and it had a huge effect on me. Because both of my parents worked, I felt I was alone, even when I wasn't physically alone. It wasn't something that was obvious to the adults around me.

I used to set the table for an extra person—for the brother or sister that everyone else had and I didn't. Every year, I'd ask for a brother or sister for Christmas.

I look back now and I think I wanted a sibling so badly because I thought that if there were someone else, my parents wouldn't always know that I was to blame when something went wrong. More important, I wanted someone who understood me, someone I could live with and understand back. I also wanted so badly to love and be loved, I thought that a sibling would help. I was already looking for outside answers to fill an inside void.

When I was young, I didn't know how to talk about how I felt; so I kept it all inside. Whenever I got upset or sad or mad, I would shut down. As a good friend says, I went into lockdown. I could feel myself stuffing the pain way down deep inside. I became very good at making it all disappear. My parents would ask if there was something wrong and I would always say no. But I could contain my feelings for only so long. The next time a stressful situation came up, I would explode. My anger would be so strong that I would become destructive and hurt myself and others.

So the cycle started early. I would shut down, contain my feelings until I exploded and became destructive. Then the self-loathing would start and I would repent over and over again. That behavior was well anchored by the time I was two.

In recovery, I can see that I behaved as an adult exactly as I had as a child. If something was wrong, I ignored it, covered it up and hid it— whatever it took to avoid feeling. When the behavior became wrapped around alcohol and drugs, it was recognizable as addictive behavior.

What I know now is that addiction is simply a behavior that covers up the disease that already exists in a person. Self-centeredness, self-loathing, alienation—these are all symptoms of a deep disease in a person. I think it varies from person to person as to what comes first. For many, addiction may be biological. They may have a chemical, biological disposition toward needing drugs and alcohol.

In my case, though, I think it was very emotional. I think the inability to understand and process my feelings as a child sent me looking for a place where I didn't have to feel them. When I found that place, when I took my first drink at 14, I was home.

TWO

Growing into Different

JOYCE: We could see that from a very young age Jamie was not living up to her potential. We would ask ourselves, "Why is she struggling so much at school when we know she is so smart? Why is she so unhappy with herself when all we can see is a beautiful, bright little child? Why is she aloof to the love around her? Why is she always dissatisfied?"

JOHN: Looking back, there was a point at which we made a decision that we would later regret.

JOYCE: Jamie was born in September. She was just turning five when she went into kindergarten at Albany Academy for Girls. Most of the other girls in her class were closer to six. In addition, Jamie was physically very tiny. Everyone else in the kindergarten class was much bigger. In fact, 98 percent of five-year-olds in America were taller than Jamie, as measured statistically.

The differences in ability between five- and six-year-olds are huge. Later in life, a year's difference in age is not very significant. In the primary years, skills such as manual dexterity, balance and coordination develop rapidly. Jamie's abilities and dexterity were not the same as those of the other kids.

One late-spring afternoon in 1977, Jamie's teacher invited John and me to the school for a parent-teacher conference. She took us out to the field where Jamie and her class were playing soccer. As we stood there, we were amazed at how small Jamie was compared with the others. Her teacher said, "I wanted you to see what a terrible disadvantage Jamie is facing here. Most of the girls are much taller, weigh much more and are physically stronger than she is. She does not stand a chance as a strong player in this game. She is too small. Her size alone requires her to be timid; otherwise, she could get hurt."

As I watched her on the field, the truth in the teacher's assessment was obvious to me. Still, I was not prepared for her next recommendation. She strongly urged us to keep Jamie in kindergarten for one more year. That would put her on equal ground with her classmates, she said. It would build her confidence and at least open the possibility for success.

I was shocked and frightened by her suggestion. I knew the teacher was right; it made sense. I also knew how highly sensitive Jamie was. I thought that even the suggestion of "being left back in kindergarten" would devastate her. She loved her classmates, and if all of them were promoted to the first grade and she did not go with them, she would certainly see it as a huge failure—one we feared would have serious consequences.

JOHN: It appeared to be a no-win situation. We felt if she stayed behind, she was going to feel like a failure; if she moved ahead, she might ultimately have problems. We didn't know how to communicate with Jamie about this. We felt we had to protect her from feeling like a failure, and we didn't know how to talk to this five-year-old about it.

We weren't trusting Jamie's abilities at all. We didn't trust her to make new friends really fast. We didn't trust that her academics would be better, even though, if we looked at it logically, she should succeed because she had already been through all the lessons that everyone else would be tackling for the first time.

But the really big thing was that we didn't trust ourselves. And because we didn't trust ourselves, we didn't trust the teacher to know what was good for Jamie.

JOYCE: The teacher told us that having her repeat kindergarten was the best thing for her. A young parent, I had no experience dealing with what I thought was my child's "failure." I wanted to protect her from the negative feelings I had when I was five. John and I had had difficult experiences in school and this situation took us back to how scared we had felt. We were looking at the situation from the perspective of our own five-year-old inner children. And we were terrified. The memory of being a tiny, confused five-year-old among giant self-assured six-year-olds came rushing back. I felt I was unsafe at school. I'd often get sick and the nurse would send me home. My mom told the school I was lying—I just wanted to be home.

JOHN: Joyce and I spent the next several months talking about what we should do. We did research, talked to educators, therapists, friends and others who had made the same decision. In the end, we thought Jamie's emotional well-being was the most important thing. But overriding everything was the fact that we didn't want Jamie to feel that she had failed in kindergarten, because we knew what it felt like! We didn't want her to feel that she wasn't good enough, because we had felt that way, and it had impacted our academic success.

Because our own early school experiences had not healed, we projected our fears onto Jamie. Through the filter of fear we made our decision. We went ahead and put her into grade one.

JOYCE: Eventually, it became evident to us that we had made a terrible mistake. While getting promoted preserved Jamie's self-confidence for a year or two, the next time the issue of academic success surfaced, all of our fears about her reaction became reality. The mistaken belief that something was wrong with Jamie would become her truth.

The Aptitude Test

JAMIE: In 1979, for grade two, I left the Academy and went to a public school. At the Academy, they had recognized the fact that I was small and young, so they coached me to help me through. That didn't happen at public school. The classes were large, they were coed and there was no special attention.

At the end of grade two, we had to take an aptitude test to assess our academic ability. Those who scored well went into the Academically Talented (AT) program. The others went into the "regular" program. I hoped that I would get into the AT program. I knew I did well in English. It was the math that I was worried about. However, all my friends *knew* for sure that they would go into the advanced program. We took the test at the end of the school year.

It was a hot day in August when the letters came. I remember it vividly. I was one month shy of my eighth birthday. We had been playing outside all day. My friends ran to their mailboxes and ran back to me with big smiles on their faces, papers in their hands, telling me to open my mail. They had all been accepted to the AT program. When I looked into my mailbox, my world, as I knew it, fell apart. There was no letter for me. In that moment, every bit of love my parents fostered in me melted away and my heart broke. That nagging voice that I had already heard in my head telling me that I was no good became even louder and clearer. "You are a failure. You are different. You are not the same. You are no good." Standing with my friends, I started to cry. I felt alone and wanted to *be* alone.

That was the first "real" reason I was different. It was the first reason with a label. I was "stupid."

JOYCE: I distinctly remember this event as having a profound effect on Jamie. That day something changed in her and in the way she related to us. It is one of those events about which, even years later, you remember all the little details. It was "the day the letter didn't come."

We lived on a small cul-de-sac where there were four girls in Jamie's class. We had all moved in at the same time when the girls were two. While Jamie spent lots of time playing with these girls, she was in a private school and joined them in public school only in the second grade. The other girls had been in this school since kindergarten. They had an understanding of the way things worked there. They all knew how important it was to get onto the academically talented track.

There was so much excitement in the neighborhood the day the successful students got the letters of acceptance. Everyone in the cul-de-sac got a letter—everyone, that is, except Jamie. She retreated to her room and sulked behind closed doors. We tried to tell her that it did not mean anything to be in the AT class, that "academically talented" was just a title. She looked at us as though we were crazy. She was obviously shattered, obviously in pain, but unwilling or unable to communicate her feelings to us. She was angry and she insisted that she didn't want to talk about it. Her dad and I sat on her bed that night, telling her how smart she was. We insisted that getting into the AT program didn't have anything to do with being smart. She just shook her head and shut herself down.

I was furious with the school system for providing no information to the parents of the students who were not in the AT program. We received no information as to how they had been tested, what the criteria were and what the implications for non-AT students would be. I tried to call someone, anyone, but the school was closed. There was no one to talk with. This was a public school system and I was told there was nothing that could be done to change the situation. In the meantime, I saw my daughter beginning to withdraw from us. I saw her become depressed and angry. And once again I felt it was my responsibility to protect her from feeling a failure. I wanted to be her shield.

JAMIE: As this was going on, I remember thinking that my parents were out of touch. Here was the proof that I was different. Why couldn't they see that? How could they deny it? That day, I took the results of that test and made the failure my reality. Everything changed at that point.

JOHN: It was a sunny day on the circle when the letter came. I remember it so vividly. I felt so bad for Jamie. I had learning difficulties in my own childhood and was so hoping that Jamie would do well and not have that same lost feeling in the academic arena. When the letter came, it took me back to my own sense of inadequacy and I became paralyzed by her pain. The only way I knew to help Jamie was to try to find a way to restore her confidence.

Looking back, I see it was another step in building our codependency. All we could think of was how to protect Jamie. We would do everything and anything to protect her, even when it was obvious to others that we weren't really protecting her at all. We were teaching her how to avoid difficult situations by not handling life's challenges.

JOYCE: It wasn't until we were writing this that Jamie told us what she was thinking that day. When we told her she was smart, that the test didn't matter, she had thought we were lying to her. In her eight-year-old mind, we were lying because we had to. She was our daughter and we wanted to protect her. That's what parents do.

How could she trust us? She knew she was stupid; the test gave her the evidence. But we wouldn't allow her to say or believe what she knew was true. What was the point of talking about it? There was nothing to say. Unknown to us until 28 years later, the keeping of secrets had started. The distancing had started. The distrust had started and I didn't have a clue that my efforts to protect her were part of the cause.

Problem—What Problem?

JAMIE: Over the next four or five years in the early '80s, Mom was working very hard at a new job, and life was kind of normal. Dad was working for the Catholic Diocese and I had moved to a coed Catholic school. It was a good school, stable, small. Small was always better for me. I felt safer, more supported than I had in public school.

For a while, the negative self-talk quieted down. I was struggling a little bit academically, but the environment was different. The school didn't make a big production of it. And I wasn't failing. I could keep up enough to be okay.

My parents knew by this time that I had a learning disability. It had not been diagnosed, but it really affected me strongly only when I had to process information, particularly when I did homework.

JOYCE: The learning disability wasn't obvious when Jamie started school. We got to it in a very strange way. We discovered it through a test for which Jamie was studying. On this particular test, the questions were all true or false. Jamie had a study sheet that had all the questions and we went through them and studied the answers.

Jamie took the test and gave the answers in the order in which she had learned them—true, false, true, true, etc. However, the teacher had rearranged the questions, so Jamie got zero on the test. We couldn't understand it. We knew that she knew the answers. How was it possible that she could get every one wrong? We finally figured out that Jamie had simply memorized the answers without connecting them to the questions. Because the questions weren't in the original order, she wasn't able to process the answers. So, in retrospect, what we were looking at was an information-processing problem.

JAMIE: There was more. I can remember being in Vincention Grade School one day when all of us had to read from a book out loud. I was having way more difficulty with it than the other kids. I felt stupid. I felt very different, and not good enough. Everyone would have to wait for me to read as I struggled. I felt so embarrassed at not being able to keep up. It was more evidence of my stupidity.

JOYCE: Jamie never shared these feelings until now.

JAMIE: It was also the time that boys and girls started to flirt. The pretty girls all had a boy or two or three chasing them. Sometimes the boys even fought over the girls. But I didn't have any boys chasing me. That was when I decided that I wasn't pretty enough. That was one more way that I didn't fit in.

JOYCE: We had no idea that this was going on.

JAMIE: So I was doing mediocrely at the Catholic school, but I was having problems with homework and processing. I always internalized everything, so it really wasn't obvious to the teachers; but my parents knew that something was wrong.

One day I came home from school and my parents said they were going to take me to this place for some extra help with school. They told me it would help me organize and do my homework better. I was furious.

JOYCE: We didn't really know why she was so angry. We were just going from place to place to find out what kind of learning disability she had. We wanted to get her help and find a name for it other than stupid.

JAMIE: I was embarrassed. The "I am stupid" story had been running in the background all these years. I said to my dad, "Only stupid people go to places like that." So I was really angry.

   They signed me up for a six-month program. They took me screaming and yelling. I wouldn't talk to my parents for hours after each session. I got nothing out of them, other than reinforcing the "stupid" story. I played their game well enough to get them to think I was doing okay. I finished the basic commitment and that was that.

JOHN: The trips to the learning center were awful. She was so angry. I didn't know how to help her with this. Only years later, at a therapeutic encounter of my own, did I realize how deeply my own "stupid" story had influenced my life and affected the way I was trying to help Jamie. Now I can see that I could not possibly have been very helpful to her, no matter what my intentions were. I was stuck in the same place she was, at the same time, only I looked like a grown-up.

JOYCE: It was hard for me to understand what Jamie's learning disability was. Heck, we took her to the experts and they didn't seem to know, either. We seemed to be confronted with a mystery and it was compounded by Jamie's anger at our attempts to get her help. Here we were, each of us acting out our own fears about being stupid, but not one of us was consciously aware that this was the underlying motivation. Without the awareness, a conclusion about it was impossible.

THREE

High School Highs

JOYCE: In 1986, we moved out of the city to a suburb. The local public school had a very good reputation. We were excited about the beautiful neighborhood. John and I were committed to public education, so we were pleased that Jamie would have access to a good education in a public school. Before we moved, she had been going to an all-girls Catholic school with small classrooms and strict supervision. She had done well there. The public high school in our new neighborhood had an excellent reputation for both academics and social consciousness. The choice we had to make was to continue at the Catholic school or transfer to the coed public school.

JOHN: We wanted, as much as possible, for Jamie to have an active part in this decision. We thought the more invested she was in the decision, the better she would do at the school.

JAMIE: My parents spoke to me about the factors I should consider. I decided to pray on it. I told my parents that God would help me with the decision. I remember, before we moved, being on the school bus that passed right by the public high school. That day, I looked out the window and saw all these handsome boys. My prayer was answered. I said to myself, "Thank you, God," and I made my decision.

JOYCE: Even though we considered all the information about current trends in education, we didn't know what was best for Jamie. But her decision was in line with our personal philosophy about education. We believed in diversity and the richness of getting to know people with different backgrounds.

JAMIE: What they didn't know was that I had already decided that I was no good; the school probably wasn't really important. I was heading down this path no matter what. But the idea of the boys' liking me was really, really important. Maybe things would have gone differently if I had stayed at the Catholic school, because boys wouldn't have been in the classrooms. More of seeking something on the outside to fill that huge empty hole on the inside.

JOHN: There was a difference of opinion regarding single-sex and coed education. One belief was that single-sex could be isolationist and it might not help kids integrate with the other sex.

JOYCE: At the same time, Jamie told us innocently that she was praying for direction. We believed in seeking internal guidance and we wanted to let Jamie know we trusted her reasoning ability. We thought either school would provide a good education, so we weren't opposed to either choice. Ultimately, we let her make the decision. The truth was, we were happy that she was communicating and seeking spiritual guidance.

JOHN: You know, looking back, it's very interesting. We had all sorts of discussions as a family about this. But the reality was that Jamie was already shut down inside, so the discussions were simply functional in nature. The real problem was that we couldn't get to the truth. We could go only so far with our conversations. We were happy to be communicating with her at all.

JAMIE: At some level, I had already moved to the place where I would say and do whatever was necessary to appease my parents. I had made my decision, so all I needed to do to get them to agree was say whatever they wanted to hear.

In the fall of 1986, I began grade nine at the public high school. That was the first of what was to become a lifetime of bad decisions. It was the first major one based on what I needed from outside to make me happy inside. The next bad decision followed very shortly after that. It was the decision to drink.

JOYCE: We had no idea how fast it all would happen. From 1981 to 1984, as executive assistant to the Commissioner of the New York State Division of Alcoholism and Alcohol Abuse, I was responsible for promoting the legislative program. We advocated for bills to reform the state's drunk-driving laws, increase the purchase age for alcohol and secure insurance coverage for alcoholism treatment programs.

At the time, the general public had little information about the effects of alcohol abuse on our society. There was still a debate as to whether or not alcoholism was a disease. Our research showed that one in ten people in America was an alcoholic. But until that time, there had not been a significant public dialogue in New York State about alcohol abuse. There was a societal attitude of acceptance for drinking alcohol that permeated our legal system, our criminal justice system and our legislative and policy-making systems as well.

In the 1960s and '70s, it wasn't uncommon for police officers to stop people for driving while intoxicated, give them a warning and send them on their way. If a person was ticketed in New York State, the average fine in the 1970s for DWI was $11. People were drinking and driving without having to pay any serious consequences.

In order to interest the legislature in making a significant policy change such as raising the drinking age to 19 in New York, Dr. Sheila Blume and the staff at the Division of Alcoholism began an educational campaign. Division staff published a research paper providing evidence to the legislature that drinking and driving was killing our kids.

The report identified DWI-related accidents as the number-one killer of people under 25. The deadly accidents were caused by a combination of the youthful drivers' inexperience, their belief that they were invulnerable and their excessive consumption of alcohol.

Dr. Blume explained that many students turn 18 in their final year of high school. Therefore, they can legally buy alcohol and provide it to their underage friends. Our research told us that the younger kids are when they start to drink, the more likely they are to binge drink or drink until they pass out. Many times they drive their cars while in a blackout state, and too often they drive in this state to their deaths. The arguments were compelling and the New York State legislature did vote to raise the purchase age for alcoholic beverages, first to 19 and later to 21.

As a result of my professional research, I was becoming aware of the effects of alcohol and substance abuse on our families, our communities and our health. But I wasn't aware of how denial, one of the disease's major symptoms, could keep so many people from seeing the truth about the extraordinary cost of addiction.

It's My Party and I'll Lie if I Want To

JAMIE: I made friends pretty quickly. I had this big personality that was attractive and I used it. I could put it on and be really convincing, really fun to be around; but that personality wasn't who I really was. I was exhibiting something on the outside that I wasn't feeling inside.

I always felt alone in a crowd, even one that I gathered around me, long before I ever picked up a drink.

People saw only the outside, though, and a lot of the kids at my new school thought I was cool. The friends I started attracting were partyers. Drinking held them together as a group. They bonded over their beer and felt part of something better than what they were on their own. When I met them, they were already into drinking and hanging out, big-time. I was, too, but the difference was that when they started to drink, they could stop. I couldn't.

The first time I consciously, overtly lied to my parents was when I started making plans to throw a party at our house when they were going to be away. I was supposed to be staying with a friend for the weekend while they were gone. My friend was very mature for her age and sounded like an adult. We decided that she would pretend to be her mom and we planned the whole party in our minds about how we were going to pull this off. We told everyone about the party on Friday.

The party started and it just grew, becoming bigger and bigger and bigger. I had just started high school, but there were seniors at the party I didn't even know. In fact, I barely knew anyone. There were people hanging out on the lawn and inside, throwing beer out the windows. It was massive. In fact, one mother came and got her daughter.

It got very out of hand. When the police were called on Friday night, it did quiet down, but there was a small group of us who stayed up and drank and partied and hung out all weekend. Despite the fact that we continued to drink, we took the car out and the party went on for two whole days.

There were thoughts in there that I shouldn't be doing that, that it was all wrong; but as soon as I drank and got drunk, those thoughts all went away. As soon as I got drunk, the lying to myself started: "It will be okay. We'll get it cleaned up. We'll replace that. My parents will never find out. We can do this. They'll never know."

But the real big deal was that people started liking me. They started accepting me. Guys were hanging out. So I just kept lying to myself and telling myself that my parents would never find out. That was when I started saying the foxhole prayer: "Please don't let them find out about this. I promise I'll never do it again."

Of course, they eventually found out that the booze was gone. It took a few days for them to get the whole story, but they did find out. Hundreds of dollars' worth of liquor was stolen and their property was damaged. I finally had to tell the truth. They were very disappointed, angry and hurt; and I was, too.

JOYCE: We found out afterward about the party. I had an interview for acceptance to the Master's in Public Administration Program at the Kennedy School of Government at Harvard, so John and I were going to be away for the weekend. We had arranged for Jamie to stay at the home of a classmate who lived a few blocks away. I spoke with the girl's mother, who assured me that she would be at home all weekend and that she shared our view on curfew time. We dropped Jamie off at her friend's house with our health proxy and a thank-you note, and off we went.

As we walked in the door when we returned home, I could feel that something was different. On the surface, the house looked clean, but as I walked across the floors, they felt sticky. A few small things were out of place. I began to suspect there might have been a party while we were gone. We looked in the liquor cabinet to see if anything was missing, but the bottles were all full—with water, of course. We don't often drink liquor, so we never suspected the vodka and gin bottles weren't full of vodka and gin. To us they just looked full.

JOHN: As Joyce said, we knew something was different. We got a call from a neighbor who told us that there had been a party. She said the police had come, and our car had been taken out by one of the kids. When Jamie came home, it was obvious that she was upset. She was sick to her stomach. She looked nervous, uncomfortable and fearful.

JOYCE: I called the mother of the girl where she had been staying to find out what had gone on. She and I had two conversations in which we discussed how it could be possible that the girls had deceived us. She waxed eloquently about how she had dropped them off at school for a basketball game and picked them up by 11. She talked about the challenges of parenting and the diligent effort parents need to make with kids.

"How could there have been a party when the girls were at your house?" I asked. "Didn't you notice that they were gone? I don't understand."

She said, "This is the first time I'm hearing about this; it's unbelievable. I dropped them off at the game and picked them up later. I can't believe that they weren't where they said they would be." She didn't miss a beat. She talked about how surprised she was that they could be so irresponsible. It was just so perplexing to both of us. Later, as I thought about the unanswered questions, I called her back. And sure enough, she had a reasonable explanation for the apparent inconsistencies in the story.

Two days later, a car drove up with three people in it—a man, a woman and Jamie's friend. The woman got out of the car. She said, "I think you think you've been speaking with me. I was just cleaning my daughter's room and I found a note that you had written to me. I now realize that you must have thought that your daughter was staying at our house." She said, "I guess you think that Jamie was with us all weekend and I thought my daughter was staying with you."

"But I spoke with you twice after the party," I said.

"No, dear," she said. "*It wasn't ever me you were speaking with, it was my daughter.*"

I couldn't believe what I was hearing. I couldn't believe that I had never spoken with an adult. Jamie's friend was brilliant at impersonating her mother. She was very mature. Her command of the English language was impressive. She did not sound like a 14-year-old; but she was. We were dumbstruck.

The entire caper had been planned in great detail. The two girls had been at our house all weekend.

JOHN: We sat down with the girls and listened to this complex story in utter amazement. Their plan had required a significant amount of forethought to pull off. I was in shock. The shock was not just about the lies, it was about how offtrack our lives had become. This was not the family I had wanted, the family I had dreamed of. This was not what was supposed to happen. What was wrong with me—with us? We were good people. We raised her well. We were loving, concerned, attentive parents. For heaven's sake, I was a therapist; it was my profession. I was supposed to be an expert in helping people with things like this. All I could think was that we didn't deserve this. I couldn't even fathom how we had got to this point. Plus, we could see the torment on Jamie's face. She was very remorseful. She was feeling bad. We could see how hard it was on her that she had conspired to have this party and had lied to us.

JOYCE: And we were worried. But it wasn't about the drinking at that point. We were worried about the choices Jamie was making. We were concerned about the lying and the scheming. Rather, John and I were focused on the lies that Jamie had told us about staying with someone else. We didn't go any further with the other problem—the fact that the kids had been drinking themselves into a stupor all weekend.

JAMIE: Mom is explosive with her anger. She explodes and then moves on. My dad, however, gets angry and then holds a grudge. It goes on for a while. But whatever their responses, the trust was now shattered

JOYCE: We were having a difficult time understanding who she was. I began to notice that my trust in Jamie was starting to break down and the foundation of our relationship was beginning to crumble. Our conversations were no longer natural and spontaneous. My thoughts became judgmental. The relationship became arduous, because everything had to be questioned. It started to take a lot of work, a lot of energy, a lot of patience to sort through the lies in the hope of finding the truth. I began to search Jamie's face, hoping to recognize the person who was my daughter.

United in Alcohol

JAMIE: We were all in it together. My friends and I definitely conspired to keep our secret. We lied to cover for one another. We would talk about what we were all going to say to make sure that the story would be consistent. But the lies were never meant to hurt anyone; they were what at the time felt like innocent lies. There was never any malice.

JOYCE: And we did check on them. They had just been caught in a huge lie, so from then on we called and went home unexpectedly to make sure that everything was okay.

JAMIE: We had no idea of the damage we were doing to ourselves—or to our families. We all knew that it was illegal for us to purchase alcohol at that time, but we also knew that we were smart enough to get it. And we were. That was when the lying really started in earnest. I knew exactly what I was doing. My friends knew exactly what they were doing.

One of my friend's brothers was 18 but looked 25. He could always supply the beer. It was easy. We all came from fairly well-off families. No one had trouble getting the cash to pay for the booze. And before we knew it, I *had* to have alcohol, particularly before school functions.

Before the Spring Fling, we all agreed to steal liquor from our parents. Then we went to one girl's house and drank it all as we were getting ready in her room. It was straight liquor—like amaretto, vodka, gin. When we were ready to go, we put gum in our mouths and went downstairs. The girl's dad drove us over to the school. He had no idea we were drunk. I'm sure we weren't acting normal, but I guess he wrote it off as our being excited.

The problem was that one of the girls had taken a Benadryl before we started drinking, because she was allergic to the cats in the house where we gathered. However, she didn't tell anyone—why would she?—so none of us knew that she had taken it.

When we got to the dance, she started convulsing; her eyes started rolling back in her head. She was vomiting. It was scary. We didn't know what was going on. We tried to carry her into the bathroom, but the teachers caught us. They called an ambulance. She was taken to the hospital, where they pumped her stomach.

We were scared and worried. We still didn't know she had taken the Benadryl, so we thought it was just the alcohol. At the same time, we didn't want to believe that alcohol could do that to us. No way.

The school called our parents. They called the police. Detectives came. They had to cancel the dance, of course, but I distinctly remember other kids yelling, "Hell, no, we won't go." Obviously, we weren't the only ones there who were drunk.

We were sent to the office and had to stay there until our parents came so the detectives could ask us questions. First I was afraid for my friend. Then all I could think about was what we were going to do to cover up. And then the tape started running—I did it again. I screwed up again. I'm stupid. I'm a failure. I let my parents down. I'm bad. What's going to happen now?

On Monday, we got called into the office. We got detention, even though we never admitted that we had been drinking. We always held fast—it was always someone else. This time it was our friend who was hospitalized, not us. It was one more nail in the coffin. Only a year and a half since I had taken my first drink—but a lifetime, it seemed, since I had started lying.

After it was all over, I became really afraid of what the consequences were going to be. I never thought about the consequences when I was drinking. I thought about them only afterward, when the booze was gone. When I was drinking, I believed there wouldn't be any consequences. Even if there were, I'd deal with them when they came, not when I was drinking. Plus, I figured that I was hurting only myself. I wasn't hurting anyone else. Self-centeredness is the core of our disease.

I wrote a letter to my parents, saying, "We're young; this is what we do when we are young. We experiment." When we found out about the Benadryl, we said, "Well, that's the problem. It's got nothing to do with our drinking straight liquor." So, even though this near-death thing had just happened, life carried on. Even the girl who had taken the Benadryl was out drinking as soon as she could.

They canceled the dance forever. They haven't had one since.

JOYCE: John went to the school the night this happened and stayed there while the detectives interviewed our daughters. The girls were only 15 and the law required that a parent be present. I was so upset that I needed some time to process what was happening. I stayed home and tried to pray, because it was the only way I knew to remain calm and rational. But my heart was beating fast and I couldn't stop the fearful thoughts from racing through my mind.

The problem was obvious to me. One of the kids was in the hospital, for heaven's sake. The police were called. The detectives were interviewing the girls. "What do you mean, there's no problem"? But everyone else was saying there wasn't a problem with underage drinking, outside of a few "troublemakers."

I was on the school principal's Advisory Council, so I put the question of what had happened at the dance on the agenda for the next meeting. Some of the other parents kept saying that it was the kids from another school who had crashed the dance and got drunk. "Not my kids," they were saying. "Not in our town." The thing was that the authorities had not revealed which child had been hospitalized, nor did they make public a list of kids who were involved, so I didn't think anyone knew.

But I told them at that meeting. I said it was our kids. It was the cheerleaders, it was the football players. "I know this," I said, "because one of them was my daughter."

No one else saw it the way I did. They probably thought I was overreacting. They said, "Kids go through these phases; they grow out of them. Didn't you?" It seemed everyone else saw this as a normal rite of passage. I knew that could be the case.

I also knew in my heart that there was something destructive happening. I knew, but I didn't know. I knew they were drinking, but I had no idea that it was as serious as it was. I felt like a lone wolf—completely alone in my intuition that something was wrong.

From my work at the Division of Alcoholism, I understood that people think that just because kids are good kids they will somehow be protected from the dangers of drunkenness. But I knew alcohol made no distinction about its deadly effect. It didn't discriminate between young and old, rich and poor, good and bad people. It was an equal-opportunity killer.

At the same time, I kept thinking that maybe I was just out of touch with what kids did these days. And that gave me some comfort. It was the only way I could stop the nagging conversation in my mind. I'd feel much better once I convinced myself that I was the only one who thought there was a problem. I stopped trusting my intuition.

I remember talking to the other parents. I said, "Our children are hurting themselves. They are drinking far more than we know. How many of you are checking them as they blow-dry their hair or are hanging out with one another in their bedrooms? You might want to, because that's when they're doing it. That's when they're drinking."

I was having this conversation with other parents, thinking that was what you did—you spoke to other people in your community. We really didn't have intimate relationships with many other parents. We did get friendly with a few of Jamie's close friends. It's interesting that none of the kids whose parents we got to know grew up to have a drinking problem.

JOHN: As I was reading the draft of this section of the book, I was saying to myself, what was I thinking? This was at least the second major event involving drinking that we knew of. We did have severe consequences from the last party. Jamie was grounded for weeks. She had to earn the money to pay for the stolen liquor. Yet denial, or the inability somehow to grasp an event that is so incomprehensible to the psyche, was taking hold of me. I wish I had acted differently. I would have imposed a major lockdown.

I was living life in past-present time and did not know it. This is an important insight into the narrative of this book. In dealing with unpleasant realities, many of us appear to live in the chronological present yet rely on skills developed years earlier with a child's rich imagination and creativity. When we are living in the past present, it is usually a result of an unhealed trauma or wound that unconsciously influences us. Thus, we are living in a past emotional time zone and a present-day chronological one. This duality prevents us from dealing with present situations entirely in the present.

I felt ashamed, just as I had when my dad's drinking caused him to repeat stories over and over. This shame was accompanied by a feeling of powerlessness. This was a familiar feeling: I had had it throughout my childhood. I now realize that this feeling of helplessness prevented me from dealing with Jamie's addiction in a more forceful manner. It was as if I were dealing with the addiction from the same helpless place of a child with a father who did not listen and a mother who would not or could not support the confrontation. I was seeing Jamie but feeling and sensing an entirely other internal reality that had very little to do with the present situation.

Do You See What I See?

JOYCE: Shortly after the episode at the dance, we found the kid in the closet. It was late on a weeknight and John and I had just fallen asleep when I was awakened by some strange noises. I sat up in bed and said, "John, do you hear those weird noises? It sounds like muffled voices coming from somewhere in the house."

"No," he said, "I don't hear anything. I think you're dreaming."

Jamie's bedroom was just across the hall from ours. It always gave me comfort to know she was asleep across the hall. Now it was strange sounds coming from her room, so I got up and went to see what was going on. She was in bed reading and I asked her if she heard voices or other noises. She said no, she hadn't heard a thing. "Are you sure?" I asked. She was tucked into her bed, looking innocent, but again my intuition told me something wasn't quite right.

Without thinking, I went over and opened the door to the little crawl space in the room. Lo and behold, there was a kid in there, in bed! She said, "Hi, Mrs. Chupka; I hope I didn't wake you."

I was so shocked to see her there; I thought maybe I was dreaming. I peered into the little space and saw quite a comfortable setup. She had a mattress, pillows, her magazines and I think a glass of milk. It looked so cozy, it almost made me smile. But I came to my senses and thought, "This is very strange." All I could think was, "What is this kid doing in a crawl space—in *my home*?

Now, we knew this young woman. She was Jamie's friend who lived around the corner. She was a great kid—sweet, respectful, adorable. What was she doing here? She quickly confessed that her parents had grounded her—probably for drinking or partying—and she had sneaked out of her house and into ours. I couldn't sustain being angry with her or with Jamie. It seemed like an innocent high school thing to do. And yet, because it was obvious that this little sleepover hadn't been approved by any of the parents, I had to call her mother at one a.m. and take her home.

I could see the love and the support these friends had for each other. I kept thinking how good it was that they had people to confide in. They clearly shared our values. I thought it was important that they were so good to each other. I was comforted by their being around our home all of the time, eating meals with us, asking for advice, offering to help with the dishes. I thought I really knew them, and I was privileged to be part of their lives in such an intimate way.

At the same time, this episode was another example of the surprising, somewhat devious, behavior that was popping up. These kids could crawl in and out of windows and live lives that we knew nothing about. And they were doing it in our homes, while we were there.

Betrayal

JOYCE: One beautiful Saturday morning, I picked up the phone and overheard Jamie on the extension making plans to go to a Bon Jovi concert. I was shocked to hear this, because Jamie was grounded at the time and she clearly knew she couldn't go to a concert. I broke into the conversation in a panicked voice and blurted out, "Jamie is grounded; she is not going anywhere."

To which Jamie calmly replied, "Oh, yes, I am going."

I dropped the phone and ran to look for John to discuss the situation. As I was calling for him, I heard the front door slam. I couldn't believe my eyes when I saw Jamie walking down the driveway with an overnight bag slung over her shoulder. My heart was beating so loudly that my eardrums were throbbing. My brain felt numb because I couldn't really believe what I was seeing. Without thinking, I took off and ran after her, shouting her name at the top of my lungs. My legs felt like rubber, but I pushed myself, running as though I were saving both of our lives. To my complete astonishment, she never looked back as I chased her down several streets. The adrenaline was pumping through my veins as I hyperfocused on my runaway child who was just beyond my reach.

JAMIE: We were running down the street and all I could think about was another lie: I shouldn't have been grounded to begin with. But, of course, my heart was breaking at the same time because I knew my mother's pain as she ran after me.

JOYCE: I was gasping for breath as we turned a corner and a car pulled up in front of us. Jamie's friends opened the car door. She got in. The sound of the car door slamming sent waves of shock through my body. I stood there completely lost in disbelief.

JAMIE: My friend who was driving kept saying, "I don't want to go. I don't think we should." I was so freaked out at that point that all I could do was scream, "Go!"

JOYCE: I heard her. The girl who was driving rolled down the window and said, "Sorry, Mrs. Chupka," as they drove away. I couldn't breathe, I couldn't think. I couldn't comprehend what had happened. My body ached. I was sobbing. I felt like Jamie had ripped out my heart and taken it with her as she pulled away in the car. I went back to the house and collapsed with grief.

JAMIE: My heart was breaking, too. It was horrible. I was in the car with my friends, and we all felt terrible for my mom. They were telling me that I shouldn't have done it. They really felt terrible for her. Of course, I came up with all these lies and justifications, but the reality was that I agreed with them. I knew what I had done; I knew what I had done was wrong; and I knew I couldn't face my parents.

JOYCE: I never could understand what gave her the audacity or the courage to keep running. I couldn't believe this was my daughter.

JAMIE: It wasn't courage, it was self-will run riot. I was going to do what I was going to do at all costs. But I felt terrible at the same time.

JOHN: When Joyce came back into the house, I felt that I had to help her pick up the pieces, to comfort her, but it was impossible. There was no way to lessen the pain she was experiencing. It was a horror. I felt as though I were looking at a scene in a movie. Unfortunately, it was our movie. I was so out of my body. It was something I never could have imagined happening in my life—my child and my wife screaming at each other, my wife running down the street after the car, Jamie in the car pulling away with her friends. I saw my wife collapse that day— she was outraged and the despair consumed her. A sense of "How could she do this?" took over. I don't remember Joyce's ever being in so much grief. I was just trying to hold her up the best I could. I was furious with Jamie.

JOYCE: Jamie had defied us. This was a notion I couldn't comprehend. While she had disobeyed us before, it had always been without our knowledge. Now I saw her defiance and disrespect clearly, perhaps for the very first time. I wanted to do something to get back my parental authority. Clearly, I had lost all control. I wanted to call the police or go to the concert and make an announcement to humiliate her. I wanted to do something to stop my pain. Our close friends came over and listened to my story. I was obsessing. I kept running ideas through my mind of how to let her know that she couldn't do whatever she wanted to.

But the truth was that she could. I felt that unless I went to get her and made her come back home, she *could* do anything she wanted. From my frame of reference, I couldn't understand how a 15-year-old could or would do these things. We had done everything we could to get her to understand the consequences of her behavior. She had been grounded, lost her phone privileges, had to do extra chores. None of these techniques had any effect on Jamie's behavior. I felt totally defeated, furious and very scared at the same time.

We waited as if in a vigil throughout the day and into the night. But Jamie didn't call. The rage and fear became all-consuming as it became clear that she wasn't coming home at all that night. Another day and night went by. We did nothing but obsessively talk about Jamie. Where was she? Who had she become?

JAMIE: We knew that the parents of one of our friends were away, so we hid out there for the weekend, partying. We drank the whole weekend, so it really numbed me out. My friends kept asking me if I didn't think I should call my parents, and I kept saying, "Not yet." The guilt was eating away at me inside, so I just drank more. The hate I felt for myself was increasing steadily; the alcohol numbed it. When I was sober, I felt. That's when alcohol began to become my safety, my friend. It numbed me. I didn't have to feel the hurt, the pain and the self-loathing.

JOYCE: By Monday, I had called all her friends. They told me they didn't know where she was, but each one assured me she was OK. I know I wasn't rational. It was the worst pain I could imagine. Finally, I called one of her friends and asked her to pass the message to Jamie that she had to come home *now*. That's when they told us where she was. One of the friends broke the code of silence. John went to get her.

JOHN: I can't even remember what happened next, I was so disgusted.

JAMIE: When Dad would get angry, he would stuff everything and he wouldn't speak to me. He was really, really angry this time. The loop started running again as soon as I saw him. I got into the car and went with him. There always came a time when I had to face the music. That's the only time that courage came into play for me. I tried to apologize, but my dad said, "I'm not talking to you right now." The silence was god-awful. It definitely forced me to "sit in my shit." I had to think then, I had to feel, and I hated it.

JOHN: I could not find the words to address the enormity of the situation. I felt betrayed, heartbroken and somewhat incredulous. I guess it was because as bad as this was, Jamie had her fabulous moments. Sometimes it felt as though we were living with two different people—this person who deeply cared about her family, friends and extended family and another who was purely self-willed—almost shut off from the effects of her actions on those around her.

Again, looking back now, and being the person I am today, I should have called the police and made a point of how unacceptable this behavior was. Back then, I was just hoping that surely she would see how this affected us and our relationship and she would stop. This was exactly what I had hoped for when my dad was drinking. I hoped he would see how that was affecting me and surely he would stop, simply because he loved me. I was wrong. He never knew the impact, because I didn't tell him until many years later.

JOYCE: We were always trying to take the high road, always trying to separate the deed from the person. So at the moment of confrontation, at the point where we would ask, "Where do we go from here?" all we could say was, "I don't understand your behavior. You've broken our hearts." And we'd all start crying.

JOHN: And then we'd have an awkward dinner. Talk about avoidance.

JAMIE: At that point, Mom would say, "Look at the choices you are making. They all involve alcohol."

But I kept going back to "It's no big deal; all my friends are doing it. It's fine. I'll be okay."

I saw getting into trouble with my parents as a consequence, but not like a legal consequence or a school consequence. I didn't see it as that big a deal. And, of course, I didn't see the alcohol as a problem.

I always thought my parents were good, better than most. And I knew by that point that I was hurting them over and over again. But the thing is, there were two monologues running in my head. In one I knew what was responsible, what was good and bad. In the other, I knew that I was bad, and it didn't matter what I did.

During this time, I did my best to be good, and for the most part, I was during the week. But when the weekend came and the drinking started, it all fell apart again. I could be good, but not all the time. Alcohol went from something I enjoyed to something I depended on.

JOHN: It was so difficult by that point to have a meaningful conversation about anything that we were like ships passing in the night. It was after this that we would see Jamie's eyes glaze over and know that there was no way we could reach her.

JOYCE: Despite all of these painful experiences, we had another side to our family that worked. Jamie could be loving and fun and caring. We spent almost every weeknight eating dinner together and sharing stories about our day.

JAMIE: We could still live our lives around the problem. We were a very good functional dysfunctional family.

What's Love Got to Do with It?

JOYCE: One of the most powerful aspects of addiction, particularly in families, is the secrecy. The secret is simple: Someone in the family is drinking or drugging. It could be the mother spiking her morning OJ with vodka, or the dad who on the way home from work every day stops "for one" that turns into four, or the grandfather who has become bitter over time and wallows in a few shots of whiskey every evening.

John's dad was an alcoholic. Everyone in the family knew it, but when they tried to speak about it, John's mom would say, "Zippa the lip! He's a hard-working man, he supports us, he is a good provider; please don't say anything bad about him."

JAMIE: In my dad's family, the addiction was covered up by humor. For my grandparents' 50th wedding anniversary, we threw a party. People told all sorts of stories. They told stories about Grandpa coming home after work and drinking boilermakers—beer followed by a whiskey chaser. The "good" part of the story was always about what Grandpa did when he was drunk. Everyone laughed. Everyone. They laughed each time the stories were told, over and over again. All I knew was that this person could drink until he was silly and everyone still loved him. So, my thought was, "If everyone is laughing, how can it be wrong?"

JOHN: Having grown up in an alcoholic family and extended family, I was so hopeful that *my* family was not going to be like that. Joyce and I weren't alcoholics, so Jamie was going to be okay. And we did talk about Jamie's problem, but I minimized it with the hope that this was normal teenage behavior. If I normalized it, the behavior associated with drinking would not seem out of the ordinary. There would be nothing to be embarrassed about or ashamed of. My dream of our being a happy family could remain intact. As I look back now, I see that I was acting from the unhealed part of me that was so afraid of what alcoholism was doing to my family. I was too scared and sad to be angry. In retrospect, I guess I was still that kid, hoping no one would ask me what was wrong. The grief the answer would bring was just too overwhelming.

JOYCE: Maybe I should have asked John to explain just what he was thinking instead of trying to convince him that there was a problem. We'd wind up arguing and he would tell me to be calm and talk me out of being too concerned.

JOHN: Even the counselors we saw wouldn't come out and say there was any significant problem.

What we didn't focus on was the strangeness of the behavior. We didn't focus on it because the behavior was somewhat normal from our family's perspective. When we had family gatherings, people drove home loaded. The next day, aunts or uncles would laugh about what the others had done. Fun was associated with alcohol. When it was time to go, my cousins and I would wave good-bye to one another while the parent drove home intoxicated. We were relieved when we were not the ones who were going home but frightened for those who were. And we never said anything to our parents or even one another about it.

JOYCE: This was so different from my family experience. When I was growing up, we talked and fought about everything. No one worried that what they said could be hurtful. When I insisted on identifying Jamie's problem, it must have sounded like I was being horribly disloyal to John's idea of family.

FOUR

· · · · · · · ·

Graduations

JOYCE: In the spring of 1989, I was awarded a scholarship to the Kennedy
School of Government at Harvard. If I accepted the opportunity to
attend Harvard in the fall, I would have to live in Cambridge during
the week and come home on weekends. This meant I would be away
during most of Jamie's senior year of high school. It was a difficult decision for me. I would be separated from John and Jamie for the first
time. As I weighed my options, I was forced to admit that my relationship with Jamie was very strained. We decided it could do us all some
good if we lived apart during the week. We worked together to create
a schedule that maximized our time together. I would come home on
two weekends a month. John and Jamie would come to Boston on
alternate weekends. I encouraged her to bring a friend when she came
to visit. I thought she would love to take a friend to a big city and
have new experiences.

Unfortunately, I was wrong. Jamie never wanted to make the trips
to Boston. John would make excuses for why she couldn't come to visit. Often I had to drive back home to see them both. It soon became an
extremely stressful time for us. Although they were very supportive

verbally, it seemed to me that they were much happier in their life apart from me. They seemed distant and uninterested in my experiences. I felt like an outsider peering into this close-knit family.

JOHN: Joyce and I were beginning to have real difficulties aligning our communication styles. The problem would become very obvious whenever we got talking about Jamie. We responded so very differently. Joyce processed situations through her emotions and I insisted on my need to evaluate them calmly. Our inability to communicate seemed to draw us farther and farther apart. We were always getting angry with each other. We were actually angry with Jamie, but we expressed it by getting angry with each other. I was frustrated by my inability to somehow get myself understood. I felt as if there were no room for my voice. It was overshadowed by Joyce's heartache, anger, fear and disappointment; and it was not strong enough to counteract Jamie's self-will. I felt a sense of despair.

JOYCE: Graduation from Harvard was one of my lifelong goals. I always felt that I needed a degree from Harvard to garner respect in the political arena. In short, I wanted the degree to prove that I was worthy of being listened to. When I came home the weekend during my final exams, John was anxious to talk to me. I took that as a hopeful sign, though he seemed different and I couldn't put my finger on the cause of his discomfort. He made an effort to have me sit comfortably as he told me in one short, emotionless sentence that our 20-year marriage was over. His words cut through my heart like a dull knife. I couldn't catch my breath at first, and then I doubled over, the force of his words striking me like a blow to my gut. I screamed and pleaded for him to wake me up from this awful dream. I barely recognized my gentle husband. How could he inflict such pain and remain so aloof? My mind refused to process what was happening, but I knew one thing: I would tell no one that John wanted to leave. If I were to speak those words, possibly they would come true. Why would he choose the week of my final exams to drop this bombshell? Was losing my family the price I would have to pay for getting my degree?

We spoke very little during the week of my exams and I stayed in Boston to pack and get ready to leave. When graduation day finally came, I was an emotional wreck. The joy and pride I felt in my accomplishment were overshadowed by the pain, confusion and fear that overtook my body and my mind. My world was shattering and the pieces were blowing all over Harvard Square.

My parents drove from Long Island and joined our closest friends in Boston the day before my graduation. Jamie and John did not arrive until the morning of the ceremony. It was a grand affair. John approached me afterward and handed me a single red rose, like the one I had carried on my wedding day. He kissed me and told me that he was sorry, but he wouldn't be staying for dinner, because Jamie needed to get home. I couldn't believe what I was hearing. Even on that day, I was not important enough to be with in recognition of this important milestone in my life. For me, it was now becoming clear that John was allowing Jamie to do whatever she wanted, at my expense. He and Jamie were now the immediate family and I was on the outside looking in. And I didn't like what I was seeing.

JOHN: The week before Joyce's final exams at Harvard, she came home for the weekend. I had been thinking about wanting to leave the marriage, because I saw no way out of the situation. I felt pulled in many directions. I was trying to have Joyce understand Jamie and Jamie understand Joyce. I was so tired of the turmoil. Joyce and Jamie were like two ships passing uneasily in the night. The trust was broken. There was no connection. It was painful to be a part of that. I had more communication with Jamie, because my denial of the seriousness of her situation made it possible. Joyce did not know how horrible I was feeling, because I could not communicate it to her. Jamie was too consumed with her lifestyle to even notice the strain that lifestyle was placing on us.

I did not know how to bring up the subject of leaving the marriage. Although I did not want to bring it up, I felt compelled to, because I saw more of the same upon Joyce's return from Harvard. Looking back, one could ask, "Why didn't you just deal with Jamie and not consider leaving?" The answer for me was that we had at least two sets of problems. The first was the difficulties Jamie presented with her lifestyle (friends, choices, relating to the family and alcohol) and the second was how Joyce and I were communicating about those problems. I did not feel as though I could be heard at all in either of those situations. I knew that my timing was absolutely horrible, but I was in such pain that I felt as though it could not wait any longer. Maybe I didn't trust myself enough to wait to speak about it until Joyce had graduated and we were together again. I thought we would just return to what was and I would be unable to express what I felt or needed. Joyce and I were completely unable to hear each other.

So on that weekend, I told Joyce I wanted to leave. She was shocked. I was shocked. We agreed to wait until after graduation to talk about what to do. Joyce remained steadfast that she was not about to let our relationship go without standing up for it in some way. She had all she could do to concentrate on passing her exams.

I did not know how to celebrate with Joyce while I was having such a hard time with our relationship. I felt absolutely miserable for causing her such pain during a crucial time in her life. I didn't know whether or not she could even tolerate my being there for the graduation while only two weeks earlier I had told her I was not sure that I could be in the marriage any longer. I did not know how to look into her eyes and say how unbelievably proud I was of her while being such an inconsiderate ass at the same time. I couldn't be with her parents while keeping a secret about what I had recently said to their daughter. While people were congratulating Joyce and saying how wonderful it was that we, as a family, were so supportive of one another, I felt sick to my stomach. I was thinking, "If only they knew." Joyce, being the kind of person she is, never let on to anyone, including Jamie, what had happened. She wanted to protect me and I suppose put it out of her own mind and heart so she could celebrate her degree.

Such a magnificent moment in Joyce's life to be tarnished by my own sense of urgency. Jamie's need to get back home for her own reasons provided an excuse for me not to deal with this major conflict of multiple emotions. So there we were, the three of us, trying to find a way to be together as well as we could, in an important moment in our family history. My desire to leave and its immediate impact on Joyce's lifelong dream is a moment for which I still have difficulty allowing myself to be forgiven. I could not get over myself to be fully present for Joyce's moment and I did not have the courage to stand up to Jamie and tell her to get over herself for a moment and notice what her mom had accomplished.

Joyce has forgiven me. I feel it is so important to recognize that, because for so long she had held that to herself to protect this image that I and other people had of me.

JAMIE: Dad's right. I was so self-absorbed and wrapped up in my sick world that no one else mattered. I had no idea how important this program and the graduation were to Mom. I now brag about her Harvard degree.

It was at this point that I was graduating from recreational use to definite substance abuse. During my final year in high school, we drank every weekend, but we had graduated from drinking at home or in the parks to drinking in bars.

JOYCE: There was an irony to the whole situation. Before I went to Harvard, I was the primary legislative advocate for increasing the drinking age in New York, first to 19 and then to 21. I was also lobbying for DWI issues to be taken more seriously—increasing the penalties and starting programs to tell high school students about the dangers of the excessive use of alcohol.

JAMIE: Ironically, my drinking at that point escalated, but my tolerance also went up. I could drink a lot more before I got drunk. So there I was, underage in a bar doing shots, while my mother was lobbying for stricter legislation.

JOYCE: What was going on was that Jamie was home with her dad. She was drinking on the weekends, but John was in denial and I didn't hear about it. I had escaped—to Harvard—and he wanted to, as well. But the only way he could do it was by denying what Jamie was doing. He was avoiding really seeing it. We all wanted to get away from one another at that point. We'd had enough.

JOHN: After Joyce's graduation and return home, we were in the midst of trying to save our marriage. We never mentioned anything about our problems to Jamie. Actually, Jamie just learned of this while we were writing this book. I, to this day, admire and love Joyce's courage to stand for what she believes in, regardless of the situation. She wholeheartedly believed in us and was willing to fight for the relationship. I was lost. I was in search of a miracle. I could not remain in the marriage as I was and I was not prepared to leave it. I had to find another solution.

Joyce's faith in our marriage never wavered. She went back to work and maintained a sense of self that indicated all was fine. She never once uttered a derogatory comment to me about what I was doing. She held space for us while I struggled to find my way. I will always love her for that. My change of mind and heart came to me through A Course in Miracles. I decided to go on a weeklong retreat and fell in love with the course. I am still its student. It remains a cornerstone of my life and has provided a great source of comfort, support and wisdom in what was to follow in my relationship with Joyce and Jamie.

When I returned from the retreat, I knew unequivocally five major principles by which to live my life:

1. All communication is an act of love or a cry for help, with no exceptions. This meant I needed to stop blaming Joyce for the way she communicated and see the communication for what it was. There are only two choices—a cry for help or an act of love. This changed drastically how I experienced our relationship.

2. The problem does not reside outside myself. The problem is in how I am viewing the situation and the meaning that I am placing on it. No exceptions. This allowed me to view my marriage differently. I could begin to stop playing an old script that says, "I am not heard" or "She does not hear me." I could be empowered to create space to allow myself to be heard. I realize I am the problem and I need only to turn it over to something greater than I understand myself to be.

3. Nothing outside myself can make me whole and nothing outside myself can take away from the wholeness I already am. This began to release the need for me to change Joyce, Jamie or anyone else for me to become okay.

4. I need to do nothing. I need only to ask. This implies an unfathomable love that the universe has for its creations. It stands ready to assist us whenever called upon.

5. We are innocent beyond what we can comprehend. This allowed me to admit to being wrong and let go of the need to be right. It created space for me to see my actions as a cry for help and to begin the process of forgiving myself and others. When we accept our innocence, we can accept responsibility for our actions. When we remain in guilt, it is more difficult to accept responsibility, because it activates our shame about our actions.

I wrote Joyce a letter while at the retreat, trying to explain what I had learned and make sense of something that was so painful. When I came home, I deeply apologized to her. She graciously accepted my apology and I began my life anew with Joyce with an entirely renewed feeling for her. I could remember her walking down the aisle in the church with a single red rose, holding her life out to me to experience and create joy.

The above principles and brief explanations do not do justice to the impact they have on my life. They continue to be my practice, at which I fail and succeed every day. They have given me a new way to experience my relationship with Joyce so that we have been able to rebuild our future together.

Broken Dreams, Broken Promises, Broken Bones

JAMIE: It was ten in the morning and a friend from high school called up and said that he had some friends out at his camp at Sacandaga Lake who wanted us to go boating with them. So we packed up, bought a 24 pack of beer—and a bit of food—and headed out.

Of course, we drank all day. In the evening, we stopped on an island and continued at a bar (even though we were all still underage). By that time, we had started drinking lemon-drop shots—straight vodka, followed by a taste of lemon. After many of those—probably 12—we got back onto the boat completely ripped and headed home. We got back to my friend's house and I discovered I didn't have any cigarettes. So I headed out to the store. It was dark and I got scared, so I started running back to the house. But because I was drunk, I ran straight into the porch steps and fell hard, landing on my face. My head bounced off the steps and blood started flowing out of my nose. It was broken really badly.

But I still didn't have the cigarettes. Plus, I was very drunk and I couldn't feel the pain in my nose. One of the guys at the house offered to put ice on it, but I wouldn't let him. And I still didn't have the cigarettes.

A friend and I hopped into the car and went off to a convenience store. I got my cigarettes, they gave me a bag of ice and I called a cab to go home. The driver took one look at me and my bloody face and said, "I've got something that will take care of that." He pulled out a joint and I thought, "Yes, this guy's an angel." So I smoked it. Now I was drunk and high.

The cab cost $80 and I discovered I no longer had my wallet with me. So when I got home, I had to run into the house to get my stash of money. Mom and Dad were sleeping.

The next morning, my father kept knocking on my bedroom door. He said, "Open the goddamn door." Now, my dad doesn't swear, ever. But he took one look at me and he said, "What the f... happened to your face?"

Remember, my dad doesn't swear, so all I could think was, "Oh, my god, I've done it again. This time I've really done it."

JOHN: We had a call from the police. They had found Jamie's wallet in a convenience store. I was so angry. It was just more of the same irresponsible behavior. I couldn't contain my rage. I just started yelling.

JAMIE: I told him everything that had happened but omitted all the drinking. He was still pissed. He said, "Get up. You're going to get your wallet and then you're going to meet your grandparents at Lake George."

JOHN: There was a family event that we had to go to that day, broken nose or not. I was looking at her and her bloody nose, thinking, "How the heck am I going to take her to see Joyce's family looking like this?" I just yelled. "Get up. Wash your face. We're going."

JAMIE: It had hurt so badly the night before that I hadn't even wiped my face. No wonder Dad was so angry. So I cleaned up and put on a ton of makeup. My friend and I went and got my wallet and went on to meet my grandparents. Thank goodness the restaurant where we met them was dark.

JOYCE: It was the first time that Jamie physically hurt herself. It wasn't the last time. It happened a lot more after that.

JAMIE: Of course, I didn't attribute the fall to the alcohol. In fact, I got really angry with the guys I was hanging out with, the ones who lived in the house where I fell. I thought they were real jerks. Somehow I managed to blame them for something that didn't have anything remotely to do with them. I was getting very, very good at totally denying everything.

FIVE

Hi Ho, Hi Ho,
It's Off to College We Go

JOYCE: Jamie had started her freshman year at a community college a few weeks before her 18th birthday. The school was a few hours from where we lived. Both sets of our parents were so proud that she was going to college, so they drove up together from Long Island to see it and celebrate her birthday. When we got to Jamie's college apartment, it was a mess. The room stank of stale beer. Empty cans, dirty clothes, rotting food lay scattered on the floor; and the girls were all hung over. Jamie was in a bad mood, belligerent. She had always been belligerent when we confronted her about her obnoxious behavior. She acted as if she were the injured or aggrieved person. She did this act so well that she would totally confuse me. I knew something was wrong, but it would become too frightening to comprehend the real problem. Maybe she was mentally ill. Maybe she was antisocial. Maybe she was just really scared and sick, unable to cope. Then I looked at the horror on our parents' faces. I was mortified. How could we be witnessing such a mess? How could Jamie not give a damn about her grandparents, who had driven for hours to see her? I was so angry that I couldn't think straight. I really couldn't process what I was witnessing.

JAMIE: It wasn't even a month into the school year when my parents came up. What they didn't know was that we had been drinking all day long, every day. We'd go to classes only when our hangovers weren't too bad. When my mom and dad showed up with my grandparents, I was hung over; but, as always, accompanying the hangover was the guilt and the shame and the pain of knowing that I was a bad person.

JOHN: All I wanted to do was lunge out of my skin and throttle Jamie. I was humiliated. I could not believe she would act in such a manner while her grandparents had made such an effort to see her. They were so proud of her. I felt ashamed, mortified and, more important, frozen. Even though this had been the umpteenth incident involving alcohol, I still felt incapable of taking action. The impact of past memory has an alarming way of disguising the present and creating the same old past results. This is important to note, because this occurred after the Course in Miracles retreat. The process of change can be slow and arduous.

JAMIE: My dad's parents never said anything—never—which made it even worse.

JOYCE: It was always like that. Jamie felt her pain to the maximum. We couldn't make her feel any worse than she did on her own. I would get angry with her about even that—she had robbed us of that twisted power over her. And, as angry as I was, it didn't seem to have any effect, because her pain was already so great.

JOHN: Jamie was feeling so rough from the drinking that she couldn't bring herself to talk to her grandparents. We went for dinner together and it was horrible. She was horrible. It reminded me of how I had felt as a kid at home when Dad showed up drunk. I felt ashamed, alone and furious. But the fury was always suppressed. My life was repeating itself, only I was now a different player in the drama.

JAMIE: It wasn't as though I went out and looked for people who drank to hang out with. Everyone at the college drank, all the time. There were days when we got up early in the morning and would see who could drink the most throughout the day—and this was after we had been drinking the night before. I won the award for the best female drinker. I can't be sure now, but I think I would have put back at least a 24 that day.

We weren't allowed to have kegs in our dorms. Of course, we went ahead and had a keg party anyway. So the school sent a note home. My dad came up to talk to me about what had happened. He stood there and talked to me with all his love. I was stone-faced. I didn't respond at all. I'd been saying "Sorry" for as long as I could remember. I couldn't say it again. He was heartbroken. He walked out and drove home. My heart was crushed. I felt as though someone had ripped it out of my chest. I'd done it *again*. I'd hurt the people who loved me the most and I was stuck with them. The guilt, shame, remorse and self-hate were unbearable. I was a wreck. But, of course, I drank that night to cover any feelings I had and just carried on.

JOHN: Jamie is right. How could she keep on doing this—after everything we had done for her, after the kind of father I thought I was? After everything good we had in our family, how could she keep doing it? I remember, as a kid and as a young adult, vowing that I would be there for my children. I knew that we would have fun together. I promised her that I would listen to her and I would let her know that she counted. I thought I would never have alcohol at the center of my life again.

I looked at Jamie and she was not there anymore. I took her vacancy to mean that she did not or could not care for me, for her mom or anyone else. It was more of the same response I had experienced in my family of origin, only without the vacant look. My hopes and desires were discounted. The drink came first. That feeling was reactivated so deeply that day. I went home a totally defeated person.

JOYCE: When John came home and told me the story, I was so angry I couldn't pay attention to his feelings. John didn't verbalize his anger. When I got angry with Jamie, he'd start defending her. It didn't add up for me, either, but I wanted to yell about it. So I did—at John.

JOHN: When Joyce started yelling, I was even more crushed. I felt as though there was no room for me to express whatever it was that I needed to express. I just couldn't cope with any of it, so I would just turn inside.

JAMIE: Although I didn't know it at that time, my drinking was starting to really affect my parents' relationship. Neither of them knew what to do with me and dealt with their anger toward me differently. But I still thought it was my problem, so couldn't understand what their problem was. Also, everyone around me was doing the same thing I was, so I didn't see it as abnormal.

My parents didn't know this, but I ended up with alcohol poisoning one night. My roommate had friends who came to visit and we started drinking hard liquor mixed with beer and got out of control. That night my roommate and I both started vomiting bile and even some blood. Then I got scared. I didn't take myself to the hospital, but we didn't drink for a couple of days after that. I don't remember thinking about it too much. I guess my brain was dead.

JOYCE: The college issued the grades directly to the students, not to the parents. After the first semester, Jamie came home with straight Bs. We thought, "Well, that's pretty good. Maybe things aren't so bad."

JAMIE: I changed the grades before I gave them to my parents. They had been all Ds.

JOYCE: We didn't find out about this until the end of the second semester. Jamie called and told us she wasn't going to go back. Finally, we got the grades and discovered that she was going to be expelled. The truth about the first semester came out at that time.

Home Again, Home Again, Jiggity Jig

JOYCE: While Jamie was away at school, we moved to a beautiful place in the country. John and I felt that we needed stillness and peace, so we bought a 20-acre place with a pond and a home with lots of windows and light. It was a bit of paradise right on earth. After Jamie flunked out of college, she came home to live with us there.

I don't think any one of us was overjoyed by the prospect of living together again, but Jamie had no money and we thought, well, at least now she was an "adult." She had lived on her own and was a responsible person.

It didn't take long to realize that Jamie was living in our home with no regard for our lifestyle. She began working during the day and she'd come home to get ready to go out late at night. We'd tell her it was inconsiderate to keep us up when we had to go to work early in the morning. She was 19; she insisted she was growing up.

JAMIE: At first, I didn't want to go home; but I still had a lot of friends in the area, so it wasn't really as difficult as it would have been if my parents had moved farther away. I didn't really want to be living with my parents. The limitations of living with them interfered with my drinking.

JOYCE: There was no peace. We'd moved to this wonderful home to be peaceful. She came home, was completely disrespectful of us and there was no peace. I became more and more resentful.

JAMIE: I did work that summer—at a camp where I'd worked for a few years. I was always able to work, despite the drinking. I could do anything with a hangover. That summer, the "I'm a failure" theme was running big-time for me. My parents were getting tired of it.

JOYCE: Yes, we were tired of it. We were tired of her playing the victim. We started talking to her differently. I was really angry with Jamie a lot of the time and it came through in my words. I was frustrated by her not being able to see her potential. I was tired of blaming her and John, and mostly I was tired of blaming myself and pointing a finger at them.

I remember a recurring conversation about who was lying. John and I saw the situation differently. The way I saw it, Jamie was doing the lying, the cheating.

JOHN: I believed it was the drinking doing those things, not Jamie.

JOYCE: John's role was always to make it better when I was upset. He would say, "Let me talk to her. Let me find out what's happening."

JAMIE: Dad was always the mediator.

JOYCE: When John would say, "It's the alcohol, not Jamie, doing all of this," I'd say:
"But who is drinking the alcohol?"
"You have to separate the act from the person," he'd say. And I wanted to believe that; so I went with it.

JOHN: To survive in my family, I had had to keep seeing the person under the addiction. I had to keep seeing Jamie different from her addiction. Over the years, as I developed as a therapist, I found a language to use that made sense to Joyce. I also thought I had to compensate for the emotional volatility

JOYCE: He was protecting both of us—from ourselves, from each other, from the reality of the situation. And I think he was offering us exactly what we wanted. The truth was that our reality was just too difficult to deal with. John gave us an out by taking care of things.

JOHN: I found it so difficult dealing with two very emotional people. I was reliving a horrible part of my childhood that I didn't want to experience again. The way I had protected myself as a child was to become very spiritual. It was the only place I could go where I could get past the pain of the loneliness and helplessness that alcoholism brings to a family. I had to look for something different, something or someone who loved me and knew what I wanted, someone who would listen and help me. That person was God. Real or not, God was who I depended on.

My dad was often drunk while he was driving us home at night from a visit to our family. I would lie down on the backseat of the car, praying that we would make it home alive. I prayed and prayed and prayed. And it worked. We always made it home. Whether or not it was magical thinking of a child, it worked and it helped me get through it. So, when the whole thing started repeating with Jamie, I prayed. I found a safe spiritual place to go to. And that's where I tried to take Joyce when she was emotional.

JOYCE: The problem was that I feared that Jamie had a drinking problem, but we couldn't talk about it. John would shut down.

JOHN: I heard Joyce. I heard what she was saying. But I had trouble with the emotion behind it, because I didn't feel that we could ever move beyond the emotion. I felt that Joyce was attacking Jamie on a personal level and when that happened, I started defending her, saying, "It's not Jamie, it's a disease." I was torn between these two women whom I loved. I couldn't find a way to bridge the gap. I also could not find the words to talk with Joyce about distinguishing the person from the disease. I felt that Jamie was always responding to the perceived attacks on a personal level. I felt if we could get beyond the person and to the disease, we might have a shot at Jamie's hearing us. I don't know if it would have made a difference. Maybe it was just my way of thinking that if we said it in just the right way, Jamie would say, "Oh, thank you so much—you are so right. Why didn't I think of that?"

JOYCE: Looking back, I think that maybe it was because I felt like an outsider. John's mom used to say about his dad, "He's a nice man, he's a good man, he has always worked so hard and made a damn good living." In fact, he never missed a day of work. Now John was saying the same things about Jamie. While they were true, she was also drinking a lot—just like his dad.

I was the only one in the family who wasn't intimate with alcoholism. I didn't grow up in an alcoholic family. I do think that when confronted with the issue of alcohol abuse, John's fear would take him back to the same coping mechanisms he had used as a child. Of course the best mechanism was denial. What made it worse was that the denial was much more sophisticated as an adult. The Beast could use its tricks of distortion to scatter the evidence that led to discovery. And John would hold on to the hope that the distortion was the truth.

JOHN: Joyce is right; the whole dynamic was getting to be familiar to me by that point. It was very, very similar to living with my dad. When you know they're drinking, you're on edge until they come home, and then all you feel is relief. The relief, the thankfulness that they are safe, takes over and you don't want to talk about anything else, because you treasure that split second of normalcy. You want your kids to be home safe with you; and when Jamie came home, she was safe, or so I thought.

Jamie was at home, but she wasn't. Our realities were so different by that point that we sometimes didn't even recognize her. The gap between us had grown so big that Joyce and I found it very difficult to have a normal conversation with or about Jamie.

Another Shot at Community College

JOYCE: Jamie went back to school in the fall of '92—to Hudson Valley Community College. She shifted her academic focus from early-childhood education to human services, and she loved it.

JAMIE: I would come home and tell my parents that I loved the addicts. As soon as I went to the human-services classes, I didn't even need to apply myself. It all came so easily to me, and that was when I knew that it was what I was supposed to be doing with my life. I got a 3.9 grade-point average that semester.

JOYCE: And I thought, "She's got it, she's finally found it. Now she can see." She finally knew that she was smart. She finally found a place to fit in. We thought we were home free.

JAMIE: I was proud of myself when I got the grades, I was really proud. But it also was a cause to celebrate. "Wow, I am smart! I deserve to go out and get wrecked." The drinking was never about going out for one drink. It was always about where I could go to drink the fastest and the most so I could get drunk

The drinking was now a reward for good behavior. It didn't occupy my thoughts all the time, but it was certainly something I did to reward myself. I wasn't drinking every day. I was able to focus at school when I had to, but the drinking would start on Thursday night at happy hour and go through Saturday night.

I was still drinking with a friend from high school, but I also met up again with a friend I had known in grade four. He was going to school at Hudson Valley, too. We hung out a bit and rekindled our friendship. At some point, he started to really like me, but I told him I wasn't interested. One night, I was out with some other friends, bar-hopping along this strip that was a favorite of ours. This guy was out at the same time and I saw him in one of the bars.

JOYCE: That night, at two a.m., we got a phone call from a man. We had no idea who it was. All he said was, "I've got your daughter and I'm going to hurt her." And then he hung up. It was terrifying.

The fear was so unbelievable that I could feel the blood pulsing through my brain and my body. We jumped out of bed and started calling every bar we could think of, asking bartenders to page Jamie. An hour and a half later, we got lucky. The daughter of a friend of ours heard the page in one of the bars and got on the phone with us. She said that she'd seen Jamie; she had been in the same bar. She calmed us down and told us she'd find her. She said she'd call us back. It was then 3:30 in the morning on a work night.

JAMIE: J came running over to the bar next door, where I was. She was hyper. She said I had to call my parents right away, that someone had called them and told them he had me and was going to hurt me. So I called home.

I eventually figured out who had made the call. It was something about what he had said to my parents. He told them they were going to find me in a garbage can. So I tracked him down the next day and confronted him and told him to back off. This guy wasn't an addict or an alcoholic; he was just sick.

JOHN: When we found out who had made that awful call, I called his father and asked to meet with him. I went over to his house and said, "With all due respect, we need to talk." I told him what had happened the night before and that I expected him to talk to his son and get him to stay away from Jamie. He was never again to be in the same place with her. His dad said he understood. It was a very firm, clear discussion. I told him that if his son came near my daughter again, I would have to take care of the situation. Now, as the reader, you need to understand that I have had only one fistfight in my entire life, when I was about 12 years old. Going over to his father's house and making this kind of threat was extremely out of character for me. However, I was persuasive, though after this situation, one would think that, as a father, I should have done something very different with my daughter. However, I was still caught up in the fear of losing her.

JOYCE: So now two things were going on. John and I had shifted to a place where we felt we had to physically step in to protect Jamie. At the same time, this incident was one more example of the craziness of the life Jamie was creating. We now saw that she was so out of control that she was attracting people who could—and would—hurt her. It was terrifying.

JAMIE: I had no idea that I was putting myself at risk with these people. It was just more bad decisions. My parents were wild with worry.

JOHN: I obviously saw that it had started to become dangerous—physically dangerous. I'm the last person who would threaten anyone, yet I had gone to this man's house and done just that. The calls in the middle of the night, along with the people with whom she was socializing and not knowing where she was or if she were safe, were taking their toll on me. I was tired. The principles I had learned from the Course in Miracles were no doubt helpful. However, I was still a student and had much to learn; and I was tired of learning.

JAMIE: They were getting sucked in, just like Carol Ann in *Poltergeist*.

JOHN: Until then, we were on the periphery of Jamie's disease. Now we were sucked into the drama and craziness of this life that centered on alcohol. We were now players in the game.

JOYCE: We had to be. We didn't have any option. Our daughter was in danger. We could never imagine being observers in a drama with her life at stake.

Bartending—the Perfect Profession

JAMIE: I started bartending at a friend's bar on September 10, 1992. As soon as I turned 21, which was the legal drinking age, I went out and got myself "the perfect job." It was great. I was making money doing what I wanted to do, and I was meeting a ton of people who also liked doing exactly what I did, which was drinking. I was making a ton of money—sometimes $100 an hour—and I got a lot of attention.

So I would go to school at Hudson Valley during the day and study what I loved, and then I'd go to my job at night and do more of a different thing that I loved. I worked hard. I never saved a dime, I never had any money, but I worked real hard.

JOYCE: I never saw Jamie drink. She never drank in front of us. So we didn't know that this was one more step of the ladder to full addiction. She always managed to hide it so well. I'd been suspecting for years but still never had the evidence. I never heard her slur her words or saw her act drunk. She was really good at hiding it.

JOHN: That we never saw Jamie drink in front of us is important. It led me to think that the problem was not as bad as I might think. Yet it was always in the background of our lives. Sometimes it took center stage and other times it loomed in the dressing room, ready to leap out at any moment. My anticipation of the next event was becoming common.

JAMIE: I knew that I belonged behind the bar. I always had a place. I also liked the control. I was so out of control with my drinking that I needed a place where I could have some control. I could cut off people's drinking. I loved it.

Crashing the Car

JAMIE: Two days after starting to work at the bar, I had a car accident. It was a night out, celebrating the perfect job. As usual, I drank too much and was in complete denial about the state I was in. I got into the car outside the bar and I backed up and hit a pole—$1,000 worth of damage in a split second. It was an expensive night. The interesting thing is that I described the whole event in my journal—but completely left out the fact that I was drunk. I simply wrote that "I got into a fender bender."

JOYCE: Which is what I remember her saying. We didn't even notice. I don't remember paying for the damage.

This illusion that addiction casts upon you is so blinding that you stop "seeing" things. You stop linking things up because you can't believe, or don't want to believe, that they are linked.

JAMIE: My friend paid for it, as a matter of fact. That was typically how I got out of something that I didn't want my parents to know about. I lied. I got guys to pay for things. I could always manipulate them to pay for anything.

JOYCE: I didn't know that, either. Had no idea.

JAMIE: It was always "Not a problem. It's taken care of." That's how I got by my parents.

Shuffling Off to Buffalo

JOYCE: Jamie graduated from HVCC in December with a degree in human services. She was going to be a day-care teacher. She did her human services practicum at a day-care center and loved it.

JAMIE: Then I did my internship at a housing project with the kids after school.

JOYCE: So I thought she was starting to mature. Now that she had the degree, she could get a better job.

JAMIE: The next step was to pursue my bachelor's degree. So I applied to Buffalo State and was accepted for January 1994. When I arrived in Buffalo, it was 50 below zero with the wind chill. It was horrible— freezing cold.

JOYCE: That was another thing. Jamie always did a lot of complaining. We were always so positive and she was always complaining. Instead of ignoring her, though, we always tried to make it better, to rescue her.

JAMIE: Buff State was so huge. There were 150 people in a class, compared with 30 at HVCC. It was tough for me. I learned much better in small classes and I was having a tough time adjusting. On top of that, Buffalo State was another party school.

One morning before class, I woke up itching. I had these red bumps. I got something to eat at the cafeteria before my first class. I went home in between and the bumps were getting bigger. So I had a shower. After my second class, I went home again and the bumps were *huge*. So I called a friend and he said it sounded like hives. "Don't get them wet, because it makes them worse."

I had a date that night, but it was cold, so I could cover up with a big sweater. We were at the movies and I went to put on some lip balm. I touched my lips and they were huge. I started to panic. We left the movie and people were starting to stare. "What is wrong with you?" So I called my mom. It turned out to be an allergic reaction to something. Ironically, it was the first time I wasn't drunk when it happened.

JOYCE: Jamie called and said, "What should I do?" I told her that she should go to the hospital. But she was arguing and said she couldn't go. I started wondering if she was drunk again. Plus, there was always something wrong. Here we thought she had gone to Buffalo and things were going well. Now we were right back to trying to figure out what the problem was this time. And I always felt that I had to have the answers. It was my job to keep her healthy and alive.

JOHN: We were as worried about Jamie's inability to cope as we were about the drinking. She was 21 years old. She had the hives. We wanted to say, "Just go to the doctor and take care of it." But there was always this drama around everything. It was totally dysfunctional.

But as much as all of that was still continuing, there was, for me, a huge sense of relief that Jamie was out of the house. We were always so on edge because we couldn't reconcile our helplessness to deal with the drinking problem we thought she had. And we didn't do that, because we still had never seen her drunk—never.

When she left for Buffalo, a wave of relief swept over me. I thought about her less. All her problems were now a five-hour drive away.

That distance can clear a lot of space in a person's mind. There was a part of me that felt guilty for experiencing such relief, but I couldn't help feeling it.

When she was right in front of us, there was nothing we could do. But there was grief, so much of it. We were sad because we saw the results of the drinking in her behavior. When she was away, it wasn't so evident on a daily basis.

The First Blackout

JAMIE: My roommate at Buffalo State was probably an alcoholic. I seemed to attract alcoholics.

JOYCE: How does that happen?

JOHN: We know how it happens—it's the law of attraction. That's very clear. We attracted this situation; Jamie was attracting alcoholics. As we look back on it now, we can see that there was some deep wound that going through this process was trying to heal. Some of that is obvious to me—healing my experiences as a child with my alcoholic father. But there's more.

JOYCE: Yes, in retrospect I can see that both of us have learned so much from this experience. But we weren't as conscious of the law of attraction back then. We weren't aware that Jamie was this powerful "alcoholic attracter," though looking back on it, it seems we must have been blind to miss it, it was so obvious.

JAMIE: Everyone I knew at Buffalo State liked to party. All of us went out drinking one night to this bar where the drinks were ridiculously low priced—something like 50 cents. I drank a lot—so much that I don't remember leaving the bar. But I did. I know I did because I woke up hours later on a bench outside my dorm. I have no idea how many hours I was on that bench, but it was still the middle of winter and it was still 50 below zero and I easily could have frozen to death.

JOYCE: I never knew about that.

JAMIE: I was scared. I thought, "What the hell happened to me?" Anything could have happened and I had no way of knowing—or of finding out. This was the most scared that I had been, and yet I still didn't think I had a drinking problem. When I went inside, everyone was sleeping, so I just went into my room and cried.

I decided that I should take it easy for a while, also that I should always stick with people. Then I'd be fine. My friends and I did talk about it later, and they said they had thought I was fine. But they were all drunk, too, so they had no idea. None of us had any idea.

JOHN: I had no idea this happened to Jamie until now. I feel horrified that this little girl we raised was collapsed on a bench in the freezing cold, in an alcoholic blackout. That image makes my heart sink. I cannot imagine how much pain she had to be in in order to completely knock herself out and almost freeze to death. I don't know what I would have felt if I had heard about this at the time. I probably would have been totally stunned, and then my heart would ache for her for having done something so totally stupid but that for us would be so totally terrifying.

JOYCE: This is, again, where we were so different. I'd go immediately to rage. There was no time for me to be sad. I just saw it as stupid, immature, outrageous! Gosh, if I didn't feel that, I would have to think of her on that bench. That would be much too painful for me to endure. The image would haunt my dreams and seep into my waking hours, filling them with sadness.

JOHN: If we had heard about it at the time, we probably would have done what we always did: We'd drive the five hours to Buffalo, we'd see that she was okay, we'd listen to her friends tell us everything was fine. But we probably wouldn't have told her, as we would now, that she had to come home and go into treatment. We kind of saw these events as totally isolated events—in a series of totally isolated events.

JOYCE: And we'd leave feeling better.

JOHN: But we didn't know about it. And on the other hand, maybe if we had, we would have insisted that she come home and enter rehab. I don't know. I know this seems crazy when you read these chapters and wonder why we didn't take action. One of the reasons is that there were so many good moments, so many times when she was not drinking—at least in front of us—that it gave us the illusion of normalcy. In alcoholic families, members often look for absolute proof that there is a problem before taking action. That is to defend themselves against the impending attack of the alcoholic who may not wish to stop.

The Buffalo Failure

JAMIE: I really worked hard at Buffalo State. I think that going from HVCC, where I got a sense that the teachers cared, to this large setting was difficult for me. At Buff State, even the study groups were large. My learning disabilities, along with the self-doubt, fear and self-hate, crept back in. At HVCC, we wrote a lot of essays and papers, at which I was good. At Buff State, it was the formalized tests that I couldn't cope with. It was like being in grade two again, when I got that zero. So as hard as I tried, I just couldn't make the grade.

JOYCE: The failure was happening slowly, but it was terrifying for me. I was afraid that she was going to beat herself up again and spiral. We had gone through all of this and she'd finally got her self-confidence after HVCC, and now it was all disappearing.

JAMIE: I lasted only one semester at Buffalo State. I felt like a failure again. All I could think was, "I'm a loser having to go back to live with my parents again. Why do I bother trying?" The conversations started up again.

JOYCE: We could see that she had worked hard. We knew her learning disability was one of the reasons. When she was commuting to college, we could help her study, but she didn't have the skills to do it alone. We could also see this destructive pattern in her behavior. But as a parent, what do you do? Where else was she going to go?

JOHN: She was our kid. We felt bad for her. We chose to invite her back home.

Conversations in Letters

JOYCE: I grew up in a house where we talked and argued—about everything. Often our discussions were passionate and heated. Often we all spoke at the same time. Often we spoke from our emotions and not from our hearts or minds. The conversations were reactive and often hurtful. When an argument ended and the anger passed, we tried to find words that would allow us to speak honestly again.

I knew how much pain the harsh words spoken in anger or fear caused my family members as I was growing up. I vowed that when I had a family of my own, I would try to speak only words that I really meant, only words that reflected the love I had in my heart. Since I am an emotional person, this was a very hard promise to keep.

Whenever something upsetting happens to me, I feel compelled to address it immediately. Obviously, this becomes an obstacle when I want to have thoughtful, information-based conversations. So, in order to have a powerful conversation with Jamie about something that was upsetting to me, I started to write her letters.

I wrote letters to Jamie throughout the 20 years of her addiction. I wrote them because I thought they would speak louder than The Beast. I wrote them because I wanted to speak my truth from a loving place, not from a place of anger or fear. I wrote them because it was the only thing I could think of to do. I wrote my letters and Jamie wrote back to me, to John and me. Jamie saved almost all the letters.

I distinctly remember the one I wrote to Jamie when she was 19 years old. She had flunked out of college and moved back home. She was staying out late at night and having trouble deciding what she wanted to do with her life. I knew she was drinking all of the time, but she kept denying it. I was deeply disturbed by her behavior, and fearful about her future. Whenever we began a conversation about her drinking, Jamie's eyes would roll up into her head and she would shut down. I would become angry and forceful with her. I was afraid to enter into a conversation with her, because we would argue and I didn't want to say anything that would give her an excuse to feel bad, give her another false reason to believe she wasn't a winner.

I was tired of the lies, the missed appointments, the hangovers she claimed were sinus infections. I was tired of talking to Jamie when I knew she wasn't hearing a word I was saying. And I was tired of the empty angry words she hurled back at me when we tried to talk. So I wrote late into the night and, with shaking hands and deep determination, I wrote this letter:

February 2, 1992

Dear Jamie,

The day you were born, our lives changed forever. Your father was so happy that he cried all the way home from the hospital. Every time I looked at you I thought my heart would burst for the love of you—I still do.

The talk we had tonight was, therefore, very hard for us because it has taken us a long time to get the courage to see things with us as they really are. I guess I always believed if I just loved you enough, the problems would go away. This weekend I finally realized I can't make them go away no matter how much I love you—only you can. The things I said tonight were the truth—they hurt me to say as much as they hurt you to hear. I want to write them down so there can be no misunderstanding, no twisting of what was said so you can feel angry and justified and make your choice based on false information.

I said you took the beer from us—it was the truth.

You said you didn't think I'd mind—that's not the truth. You know how I feel about it and if you thought I'd say yes, why didn't you ask?

I said you come into my room and take my things without asking. When I ask you, you say you didn't take them. YOU DO TAKE MY THINGS without asking—that's the truth. When you say you didn't take them, it's a LIE.

I said you spend a lot of your time focusing on alcohol. You said you don't. Maybe you believe that, but I don't. I know drinking every weekend more than one or two can lead to real emotional problems, because alcohol is a depressant. It makes you feel insecure and alone after you stop drinking and when you

feel happy and ready to party, THAT'S THE TRAP. Alcohol
lies. It lies so much that it's hard to know what the truth is after
a while.

Let's get one thing straight here and now. The love, support
and material gifts we have given you were given out of pure
love. WE DO NOT EXPECT YOU TO FALL ON YOUR KNEES
DAILY IN A FALSE SHOW OF GRATITUDE.

We do expect you to return our love and act as if you respect
us and our limits. Actions speak louder than false words of
tribute. We expect that you recognize the difference between
what is yours and what is ours—you are old enough to know.

You are hurting yourself when you delude yourself into
believing that you have somehow been mistreated by us. Jamie,
the only one mistreating you is you.

You hurt yourself when you choose to give up your power to
the God of Fear. It hurts your growth when you don't believe in
yourself, don't honor who you are. You hurt yourself when you
choose that which feels good at the moment over what will be
best for you forever.

You hurt yourself when you say you don't know instead of
knowing that you do. It's very hard for us to watch this over and
over without somehow bringing our part of it to an end.

It hurts us to think we say all this and you may choose not
to understand. You may choose to turn things around and think
we are somehow making you suffer. That's not true. It's you who
you are hurting.

What is true is that it's time for you to decide that you are
going to make some changes in your life. It's time for you to
decide to tell the truth to yourself and to us. It's time for you to
start loving and respecting yourself as much as we do you. It's

time for you to start learning your boundaries, to know your priorities and stick to them. We hope you'll choose to do that here where we can offer support and comfort.

If you decide to leave in these economic times, you will have chosen a road that is long and hard. It will eventually lead you home having made the changes by a much more difficult route. But, make the changes you shall. Because that is just part of growing up.

We are loving you while you make your choice. Mom

JAMIE: My parents and I had developed a type of letter relationship over the years. Most of our important, intimate communication was through letters.

When I received this particular letter, I was already a full-blown alcoholic. I had already begun to drink every day. So it wasn't the first time that Mom confronted me about my drinking, but it was different from other times. It seemed to me that she had had a type of epiphany. I remember thinking, "Wow, she really does know what's happening."

Mom said the choice was mine alone to make. She said that she and Dad would be loving me as I made that decision. But she was very clear that it was my decision and that I was making it alone.

As I read, part of me wanted to run, part of me knew that Mom was right. I would never change. I would never be a success; look at my record thus far. But I was so far gone into my addiction that my lying and denial won out. I dismissed the letter. I disregarded the plea my mom was making. I listened to the lies. I listened to my self-hate, that inner voice, tell me I was no good.

JOHN: I remember when Joyce wrote that letter. She showed it to me before she gave it to Jamie. I wrote letters to Jamie as well, many of them. For me, they were a way of maintaining contact when it was too difficult, painful or simply impossible to have a conversation with her. We reverted to letters, even when we were living in the same house. I suppose letters also were an easier way for me to say what I had to say when it was impossible for me to have a difficult conversation. Again, we come back to the communication pattern of the untreated child of an alcoholic.

JOYCE: That letter was one of the most powerful I ever wrote to Jamie. It came from my heart. It came from my fear. I wrote it because I could not say the words I needed to say. I was so upset, so disturbed by her behavior, that I could not express what I was seeing any other way. It was an attempt to communicate to Jamie that she wasn't fooling us, that we knew what was happening with her.

JAMIE: It was as though there were a very high brick wall between us. The wall was so high and we would all get so upset that my mom and dad couldn't find a way to climb over it. But they could write a letter and toss the envelope up over the wall. If it landed on my side, they knew I would read it. They knew that I would read it, that I would read and reread and reread the letter. They knew that I would pay attention to their words if they were written down.

JOHN: Jamie's commitment to denial did not allow us to have any conversations with her about alcohol. She would completely shut down. She would go into a coma-like state, stare at the floor or the wall and wait us out without responding.

JAMIE: The letters did work to some extent. When I read them, the feelings would come up. I was using so that I didn't have to feel. When my parents talked to me in person, I chose not to respond. But I couldn't avoid responding when I read the words.

JOHN: The face-to-face conversations would get so difficult—Joyce would be so emotional and Jamie would be so shut down—that nothing good would happen.

JOYCE: When I put my thoughts down on paper, they couldn't be misinterpreted. There they were in black and white. There couldn't be any "Well, you said . . .!"

JAMIE: Sometimes, even now, I show my parents' letters to my clients who are struggling with children in addiction. I think all of us would suggest to families who are in the throes of addiction to write letters when they find that they can't talk anymore, but to be sure to read them before they give them to the other person!

JOHN: The other benefit I got from the letter writing was that it created space for me to listen to myself. It allowed me to hear my heart and mind. It spoke to the power of the word. I think I knew, at some level, that she would read the notes and it would have impact.

JOYCE: It was also a way of taking action when no other action seemed possible. It gave us a way of doing something to try to influence Jamie. We wrote letters to her all the way through her addiction. They were a physical reminder of our loving support.

. . . .

SIX

Winner Take All

JAMIE: In January 1998, I was working three jobs: I was a secretary at the New York Senate, a bartender at Ziggy's two nights a week and at a sports bar on Sundays from 12 to 8. I had gone to Myrtle Beach for a holiday and loved it, so I was saving my money to move there. I started seeing a therapist on January 19. I was depressed.

JOYCE: On February fifth, the three of us won the Superbowl Square bar game for $4,000. We gave $2,000 of the winnings to Jamie.

JOHN: When I shared the news with one of our friends, she asked, "How come Jamie got 50 percent of the take when there were three of you in the game?" The sad part about this was that we didn't even think about that. Codependency is an insidious behavior pattern.

JOYCE: Jamie then had all this cash. She decided that she would quit her job at the state senate and move to the beach. She expected us to argue with her against that; but we thought the move to Myrtle Beach was to enroll at the University of South Carolina to finish her degree. How could we not support that?

JAMIE: My friend K—the one who had her stomach pumped at the dance in grade ten because she had had the Benadryl—was living there, making $40,000 to $50,000 a year at a good job. I was going to move in with her.

JOYCE: Once again, we were in complete denial. I mean, K! Of all people, this was the person she should not have lived with. But K was now very responsible. She was doing very well. We convinced ourselves that the move would be good for Jamie. It would force her to take care of herself, to grow into a responsible person. Honestly, we also needed some relief from the constant worry about her lifestyle and her well-being.

JAMIE: I wrote a letter to my mom and dad that was filled with love and hope and expectations. I really was looking forward to this adventure. I had the best intentions—I always had an honest desire to do what I said I was going to do. I wanted to get my degree; I wanted to be successful.

When I got to Myrtle Beach, I was going to enroll, but in the meantime, I got a job bartending. I needed to make money for the rent. The bar was a biker bar. I was making good money—$300 to $400 a night. And when the annual Bike Week came, I was making a grand a night in tips.

Then I got another bartending job for Sunday nights. So now I was working at two jobs, six nights a week, making $400 a night. That was, like, $2,500 a week, well over $100,000 a year.

At the same time, my drinking increased dramatically. I was drinking every night. I would drink at work until the bar closed. Then I'd sleep in to three in the afternoon and then get up and do it all over again. My life was very simple and predictable.

One night, a customer said to me, "I've got something for you." It was a vial of coke. I had done coke one other time, but I hadn't liked it. Everyone who worked at the bar—there were three of us—started doing lines. This time I got the effects of it. There was a lot of coke.

The three of us always worked together and the coke thing became a habit. Every night. We were making more than enough money to pay for it—no problem. My boss at the Sunday-night bar was also a cokehead. It was everywhere.

Then I started dating a dealer and it all became simple.

I had friends there who only drank and never did drugs. They started asking me what was wrong: Why was I losing weight? Was I sick?

One night, my boyfriend, the drug dealer, and I went to an after party and continued. And I always wanted more. At one point, he looked at me and said, "Wow. Enough is never enough for you, is it?" And I was shocked. I realized it was true, but I didn't know how to stop.

The reality was that I knew when I was bartending that I had a drinking problem, but I joked about it. I knew if I took it seriously, I'd be in trouble.

JOYCE: About that time—it was May of 1998—I drove my parents down to Florida. They were both critically ill. My mother had cancer and my dad had congestive heart failure. On my way back, I stopped to visit Jamie in Myrtle Beach. It was Mothers' Day. She booked me into a really wonderful hotel.

After dinner, we went to the bar where she was working. They were all drinking a lot. It was upsetting me so much that I left and went back to my room. Jamie didn't get back to the hotel until four or five the next morning. This was supposed to be our time together and she stayed out all night. She knew I had to leave the next morning, but she was wiped out from partying. I told her I wanted to visit with her, so she got up and we sat on a blanket at the beach trying to communicate. She was so distant and exhausted. I told her how worried I was about her, but she insisted she was better than she had ever been. She talked about registering for school and saving money. I searched her face for the daughter I loved so deeply but saw a stranger looking back at me. I left her at one in the afternoon, sleeping under a blanket on the empty beach.

I drove away consumed with worry. Thoughts of grief were filling my head. Then I thought, still, I hadn't seen her drunk.

JAMIE: She did make a comment, though, that she was concerned about my lifestyle.

JOHN: Joyce was beside herself when she came home from that trip. She was devastated by this experience. She had driven out of her way to see Jamie in Myrtle Beach, hoping that she would get some time with her.

JOYCE: It was three and a half hours each way from the interstate to Myrtle Beach, so I drove seven hours total. And what I found was a party girl who had no time for me. There was a total lack of connection, a total lack of sincerity from Jamie.

I was always couching my words to Jamie. I didn't want to be the nagging parent, so instead of saying "What the hell are you doing? Stop partying and spend some time with me!" I'd say, "I'm concerned about your lifestyle." It always seemed to put the issue even further underground. The more frequently we avoided, the bigger the avoidance became and the bigger the block to confronting it became.

JOHN: I felt so terrible for Joyce. She could not even convey the depth of how bad she felt—how utterly crushing it was to have your daughter be so involved with her lifestyle and drinking that she could not extend herself to her mom. It was another divide in the relationship. I survived by not feeling as much. I distanced myself from Jamie's situation. We had our life, our responsibilities, and I needed to carry on in some normal fashion. In some way, it kept me sane.

JOYCE: She was 25 years old. What could we do?

JOHN: What we did know, though, was that we couldn't count on her—at all.

Descending into Hell

JOYCE: On the Thursday morning of the 1998 Labor Day weekend, the phone rang at 6:30 a.m. I awoke, startled, and answered it. Silence. No one was there.

In a split second, all the nightmares of the previous years rushed through me. I said to John, "Something is wrong with Jamie."

JOHN: I knew it was Jamie, too. We tried to call her, but there was no answer at her apartment. She didn't have a cell phone, so there was no way for us to locate her. We felt uneasy as we left for work.

JOYCE: There was nothing to do but carry on. We had no real reason to think something was wrong. It was just an uneasy feeling. But we were familiar with that kind of feeling. I went to work at the Department of Health and John kept his appointments with his clients. We were both on edge all day. I had just gotten in from work when the phone rang. It was Jamie. She was sobbing hysterically. "I've been raped," she said.

I can still remember exactly where I stood in my kitchen as she spoke those devastating words. A million thoughts rushed through my brain. I tried desperately to think of something to say that might comfort her. "Oh, my god, I am so sorry, Jamie," was all I could utter. I said it over and over as she told me in graphic detail about the violent assault on her body and her soul.

JAMIE: By then I had broken up with the drug dealer and I was kind of hanging out with the manager of the biker bar. He was 20 years older than I was. One night, he and I were fighting. I was working, I'd had a couple of drinks and I wanted to find some drugs. I knew someone at his house had them and I was going to go there to get them. However, I wasn't sure where it was.

We closed the bar, I got into my car and I started driving around, looking for his house. I pulled into a gas station. There was a guy talking on the phone in one of those outdoor telephone booths. As soon as I drove up, he hung up and walked over to the car. I asked him if he knew where this apartment block was, and he said, "Yes, I can show you where it is." So I said, "Come on and get in."

He got into the car and I started driving and driving and driving, and he finally said, "Take a right here." He told me that he knew someone who could get us coke.

We ended up in a wooded area with a dirt path just big enough for a car. There was a light in the distance. He got out of the car and started calling for Mario. I thought his friend must live in the bush somewhere. Finally, he said, "Get out of the car."

I got out of the car. He said, "Take your pants off."

I said, "*No.*"

He said, "Do you want to get cut?"—he'd pulled out a knife. So I just did what he told me to. But I wasn't in my body. It was like I was sitting on a branch way up high in a tree. He raped me on the hood of my car.

———————

Afterward, we got back into the car and we drove for a bit and ended up at a chain-link fence. It was 5:54 a.m. He got out and left me and said, "If you leave, I will find you and kill you."

So I kept looking at the clock and said I would wait until 5:57 a.m., just long enough for him to be far enough away. At 5:57, even though I was terrified, I took off. I kept looking in the rearview mirror to see if he was following me.

I drove to my apartment. No one was there. I called my parents— that was the call at 6:30 in the morning—but I couldn't talk. I wasn't even in my body. I was so traumatized. I pulled the blinds shut. I didn't want to leave my apartment. I still thought he would come and find me. Eventually, I called someone from home and told her what had happened. She said, "Did you take a shower?" I said no. She said, "Don't take a shower; leave your clothes on and go to the hospital."

I drove to the house of a guy I knew and trusted. He took me to the hospital. It was raining that night. They did a whole rape kit on me. I filed a report with the police and then went back to my apartment. I was in utter shock. I didn't know what to do. Thank God my friend was there. He was helping me through this. I couldn't bear to think at all.

JOHN: I was watching Joyce have this conversation with Jamie, but she was talking without breathing. All I could hear her say was, "I'm so sorry, I'm so sorry." She was trying to communicate to me while she was talking to Jamie, but I wasn't sure what was going on.

JOYCE: She was hysterical. It was all I could do to keep it together. We told Jamie we'd be right there.

JOHN: When Joyce got off the phone, I tried to comfort her and then started working out how we would get to Myrtle Beach. There was no time to feel anything. We just had to spring into action. We had to take care of the animals and close up the house. We also had to figure out how we were going to stay up all night, because it was a 16-hour drive.

At 11 p.m., we got into the car and started driving. We drove through the night and hit the mountains of West Virginia as the sun was coming up.

JOYCE: You know, one of the interesting things was that when we were going through those hours, we didn't focus on the idea that this was related to alcohol.

JOHN: I'm not so sure. I thought about it. It was in the back of my thoughts, but it was not the time to even question it; nor do I think we talked about it together. We kept trying to focus on the positive—she was alive, she was not cut or physically damaged. We weren't going to the coroner's office to identify her body.

But I was also angry—angry about her lifestyle, angry and scared she was knowingly or unknowingly placing herself in dangerous situations. I was trying to find a place for our anger along with our desire to be supportive. The rape, as it should have, overshadowed any critical feelings that we might have had at that moment regarding her lifestyle. In the midst of all this horror, we concentrated on a loving presence that was supporting us individually and collectively as we went through this. Both of us could absolutely feel the embrace of the unknown hold us, support us and reassure us.

JOYCE: That week, a plane had crashed over Long Island and people were going to identify the bodies. It was a backdrop to our own personal experience. As we drove, we were listening to the reporting on NPR about the families going to identify the bodies. At one point the next morning, John and I stopped to watch the beautiful sunrise. As we sat quietly, we both became overwhelmed with gratitude that we were going to be able to see Jamie alive. That helped keep the rage, the terror, the concern and the helplessness contained.

We talked about how we could use our spiritual beliefs to get us through this next event. I remember at one point, while we were talking, having this overwhelming feeling of safety and love in the midst of this tragedy. We talked about how our gratitude that she was alive helped us understand what grace was. It was from this place that we would be able to give unconditional love to our daughter. It was the only tool we had to help her heal.

JOHN: And it was what we chose to focus on. All I knew was that I wanted to be totally present for Jamie and Joyce. I did not want my anger or vengeful thoughts about the perpetrator to take up any space in my consciousness. I desired more than anything else the love of the entire universe to pour through me as I got ready to see Jamie.

JOYCE: I just didn't want to give him any energy at all. So I was quite conscious about not giving him any space in my thoughts. I gave him over to God. I said, "There isn't anything I can do with this guy. This one is God's job."

We finally arrived at five p.m. on the Saturday, now a day and a half after the rape. We opened the door and found that the blinds were pulled tightly closed. It was hot and dark. I thought to myself, "This must be what hell feels like."

When we walked into Jamie's room, we found her in a fetal position under the covers. We could hardly recognize our child. Her face was distorted and swollen. She had been crying for almost two days. She was so traumatized. We sat on her bed and just held her and rocked her while we wept together.

JAMIE: Shortly after my parents arrived, the doorbell rang again. It was the police. They had checked my car the day before, but because it had been raining all day, the car was clean. No fingerprints. No evidence, even though it all happened right on the hood. They were there to tell me that. I had the blinds shut, was in a fetal position on the couch. I couldn't move. I couldn't put a thought together. I couldn't eat, I couldn't drink, I couldn't do anything.

JOYCE: I walked outside with one of the policemen. He said, "You know, ma'am, I've seen this happen so many times. Beautiful, innocent girls like your daughter get caught up in this illusion, this Tinseltown, and they get in trouble." He said, "If it were my daughter, I'd take her home." But it took two days to persuade her to go.

JOHN: Sunday night, Jamie wanted to get out of the apartment. We thought it was a good idea. Some of her friends, including her manager, who was to be her future boyfriend, went with us. We went out for dinner and they all, including Jamie, started drinking. Shots. Much more than just a little glass of wine. I don't know how to describe that night. I think Jamie wanted to go out just to prove to herself and the perpetrator that he was not going to take her life away. She would still stand. She was, in some way, I think, trying to reclaim whatever part of herself she could. I followed her like some protective bear, ensuring her safety, trying to protect her from harm while she coped with a violent intrusion upon herself the best way she could.

On the one hand, I knew it was insane to go out and have dinner, but on the other hand, I also knew it was important for Jamie to do something—anything—to reclaim her being. This was not the time for us to control what she was going to do, given the fact that she had experienced something horrible beyond her control.

JOYCE: It was a restaurant bar. The boyfriend asked me to dance. I said, "You know, alcohol is the worst thing to do right now."

He said, "Well, I'm just trying to help her get on with her life."

I said, "Partying is not the way that she is going to deal with this. It's not going to help her get on with her life, it is what is *stealing* her life."

JOHN: Those three days in Myrtle Beach were like an eternity. Our daughter, curled up in a ball, was totally collapsed within herself, feeling a brokenness beyond what we could ever imagine. She was trying to decide what to do and where to go. She knew she couldn't stay and we knew she couldn't stay. She couldn't say it, so we said it for her. I know Jamie walked out of the apartment on her own two feet with her belongings in tow. However, it felt as though we were picking up the fragments of her bones. We gathered her up into our arms, held her close, breathed life into her and gently placed what was left of her in the backseat of the car.

JOYCE: It took us 20 hours to get home. Jamie couldn't do anything by herself. She was shaking in the backseat like a little rag doll wrapped in a blanket. She was hardly recognizable; she wasn't speaking, she was completely broken.

JAMIE: I started to have panic attacks. I was petrified to go anywhere outside the car by myself. I even made my mom go into the restroom with me.

JOYCE: We sang songs to her and cried with her and brought our wounded child home. It was a few days before her 26th birthday.

JAMIE: When I came home, I went to a rape crisis center. They were okay, but they wanted me to do things like "color my feelings." That type of therapy didn't work for me. But it did help to have someone identify with me, someone who knew exactly what I was feeling, what I was going through and what I was to expect.

JOYCE: Almost immediately, Jamie started hanging out with an old friend of hers—who was an alcoholic. I remember saying to John that we had to talk to Jamie about hanging out with her.

JOHN: So one day, in front of this person, Joyce said, "Every time you get into trouble, alcohol is involved. Drinking is making all your decisions for you, and they are not good decisions."

JAMIE: I stood up and said to my parents, "Are you telling me I'm an alcoholic?"

JOYCE: I said, "I don't know; maybe you are. But certainly drinking is getting you in trouble." She stood up in her righteous way and she left the house. Every time she left, there was the worry that she wouldn't come back, that she would get hurt. I wanted to run after her and take back what I had said.

JAMIE: I knew full well that the rape had happened because of the drinking and the drugs; but the denial was so strong that all I wanted to do was take the pain away. Before the rape, I drank to feel better, to feel prettier, to feel accepted, to feel smart, to feel funny. After the rape, the only reason I drank was so that I wouldn't have to feel.

———

Today, as I talk about the rape, I'm recalling it. When I used to talk about it, I was reliving it. I started crying as I wrote this story again this time. I had to go to the washroom to take a break. I thought to myself, "I really don't like having to recall this, but it's important. I know it's important, because so many people—guys and girls—get raped when they are drinking and drugging. And so many of them can't get themselves beyond that point."

They say in recovery that if the drugs don't kill you, the lifestyle will. It's true.

JOYCE: I was always grieving for my child whom I never knew. Now, in the recalling of the story and working on this book, I am so grateful for getting to know the beautiful, intelligent woman my daughter has become.

JOHN: The unspoken thing was that we all knew that alcohol and drugs were a major contributing factor to the rape. But the trauma was so strong at that time and she was not in any treatment setting where we could talk about it together in a safe manner without risking further harm. We believed Jamie was always punishing herself much more than we could. But that was not spoken; the secret was getting more and more insidious in our lives. What went unsaid was creating a hell on earth.

SEVEN

Southern Exposure

JOYCE: While all of this was going on, my parents, to whom we were extremely close, were beginning to need much more help. My dad had congestive heart failure and my mom was in the fourth stage of colon cancer. He couldn't breathe. He was so weak he couldn't continue to care for himself and the apartment. She didn't know how to drive, and they spent their days going from one doctor to the next. We were consumed with worry because they were in Florida, thousands of miles away from us, so we couldn't just stop in to check on them. It was becoming clear that they were getting too ill to take care of themselves. I was a few years from retiring, so leaving my job to care for them was not a viable option. They were unwilling to come to upstate New York and live with us, since none of their doctors or community of support other than us were here. Once again, I was trying to figure out how to make everyone's life better. Actually, at this point, I just wanted to make their life livable. Then I got what I thought was a brilliant idea. It could be a solution to both of my problems. Jamie didn't have a job, and my parents needed help. Perfect: Jamie could go to Florida to live with my parents. She could grocery shop, cook for them and take them to their doctors. Plus, she didn't like the cold, and winter was setting in. This was a way for her to get all the things she needed and to help my parents, whom she loved dearly. So Jamie went down to West Palm Beach and stayed in my parents' two-bedroom apartment.

It hadn't been a month when I got a call from my dad early one morning. He was crying. I said, "What's wrong? What's wrong?" I thought maybe something had happened to my mom.

He said, "Jamie is in jail. She was arrested last night for a DWI."

In jail? I never knew anyone who had gone to jail. I could not be hearing this correctly. But it was true. I was so outraged, enraged, in a rage in general. I can't even tell you the emotions that were in my body. They weren't even in my mind, they were in my body. I said, "Leave her there; leave her in jail."

He said, "I can't. She's my granddaughter. I can't do that."

JAMIE: I knew my grandparents were sick and I really wanted to help them. I never had any intention of sabotaging my family. I never set out to say, "I'm going to hurt my family." No one ever says, "I'm going to grow up to be an alcoholic." I really wanted to help my grandparents.

So I packed up my car and drove from Albany to Myrtle Beach with a U-Haul. The manager of the biker bar where I had worked in Myrtle Beach helped me load up my stuff, which was still in storage from after the rape. I drove to Florida by myself. I was going to help my grandparents.

JOYCE: She was going to go to college once she got to Palm Beach. Her grandparents had done all sorts of research for her. She was going to continue with her education.

JAMIE: I got to Florida. I was helping my grandparents a little bit, doing what I could. I wasn't drinking a lot there. I was still drinking, but it wasn't every night.

Then my former manager started sending me joints in the mail. And every once in a while, I would go out and drink, but not excessively, or so I thought. Probably I was legally drunk every time, but because it wasn't all the time, it seemed okay.

One night, I met a guy in a gas station. We went out that night to a bar that was close to my grandparents' apartment.

JOYCE: Think about that for a moment. She had just gotten raped by a guy she met in a gas station. Now she's going out with another guy she met in a gas station. It didn't make any sense.

JAMIE: I had maybe three or four beers with this guy. Then we went to another bar and I had two drinks and I blacked out. I think someone must have put something in one of my drinks, because I could drink 20 drinks, 17 shots in one night, no problem. I remember putting my key into the car, and then I blacked out.

When you are in a blackout, you are awake, and you do whatever you do, but you don't remember any of it. It's a temporary memory loss, and you never get that time back. You're killing your brain cells.

The next thing I remember is waking up and this guy, who was in the car with me, saying, "Take the key out of the ignition, quickly." He thought that if we were pulled over and the key wasn't in the ignition, we weren't technically operating the car.

But hello—the windshield was crashed. I had hit a pole and his head had gone through the windshield.

The cops gave me a field sobriety test and I failed that, obviously. They took me to the station and booked me. I was put into a holding cell.

I remember, when I came out of the blackout, sitting there, thinking, "Let's call 911"—always in denial, always trying to minimize things, being stupid. I don't think I even knew at that point that I had totaled the car.

It was always "How am I going to get out of this one? What kind of lie am I going to make up to get out of this?" Part of it was keeping the denial going, but a big part was not wanting to hurt anyone.

JOYCE: You didn't want to hurt your grandparents. We know that.

JAMIE: The jail officer came to get me and said, "Your family is here." My heart just sank. My grandfather and I rode upstairs from the cells in an elevator with a couple of people who had been in the cell with me.

One of the officers said, "Someone needs to go home and take a shower." It was me. I stank of alcohol so badly that other people could smell it.

JOYCE: But she had only three drinks.

JOHN: I remember the call. I could not believe what I was hearing. I was dumbfounded. I told Joyce's dad not to bail her out. We weren't going to; neither should he. We couldn't do this again. If he wanted to do it, that was fine.

JAMIE: I still don't know how my grandparents found out.

JOYCE: Dad went down to get her. I said to him, "I am so angry with her that you have to give me a few days; I can't speak to her." I said, "I'm really, really sorry that I have to put you through this, but I cannot speak to her."

"But," he said, "she looks so awful and she's so sick." He didn't know everything that she'd been going through, that we'd been going through. It was all part of our group denial.

Jamie had started telling the story that someone had put something in her drink. This is the point where I had just had enough. I'd had enough with the lies, with the disregard for anyone else. When it was just my child and I, it was one thing; but when she pulled my parents into it, I couldn't deal with it.

JAMIE: But didn't you know I would drink again?

JOYCE: More denial. I really had convinced myself that you wouldn't. You had promised that you weren't going to drink in Florida. You were recovering from a rape. You were going to go to college. You were going to do something noble, caring for someone else.

JOHN: Looking back at this situation now, I realize how little we knew about the seriousness of addiction and how it can cloud the judgment of best intentions. I did not grasp the extent of the hold alcohol had on Jamie's life. We made a serious mistake in judgment in thinking she could go down and be with her grandparents to help. First of all, she was still dealing with the trauma of the rape. Second, she was very close to both grandparents, and to see them sick, while she was still trying to deal with her own issues, could not have been easy. Third, and most important, she was still active. We thought that as a non-addict or a person not afflicted with the disease of alcoholism, if you loved someone, you would do whatever it took to be there for him or her in a time of crisis. We did not consider that The Beast has only one desire, and that is to feed itself. It cannot see past that. My own denial had a serious impact on my reasoning judgment.

JOYCE: What were we thinking? We thought we were helping boost her self-esteem. We thought that by giving her the opportunity to do something "noble," she would gain her self-esteem, and that would help her reclaim her life.

We also know now that we knew nothing about Jamie's type of addiction. We weren't going to Narcotics Anonymous (NA) or Alcoholics Anonymous (AA) meetings. We weren't talking to anyone else who had the same experience. We never knew anyone who went to AA.

The alcoholism that we knew with John's dad was very different. He was a functional alcoholic. He went to work every day. He always showed up for his responsibilities. He took care of his family.

JOHN: We were taking a rational, logical approach to try to understand what was happening. We were constantly trying to figure it out.

JOYCE: The truth was that there was nothing to figure out other than what went without saying. Alcohol and drugs had taken over Jamie's life and until she realized it and wanted to change, nothing would change.

JOHN: We also thought the power of love was stronger than the power of the addiction. We forgot that the person first has to say yes to the love of self in order to experience its power.

JAMIE: When I saw my grandfather and grandmother at the jail, I was scared. They just picked me up, put me into the car. They didn't say anything to me. When we got home, my grandfather finally spoke. He said, very simply, "You can never, ever drink again."

I said, "I know." The failure *again*. The one who always let everyone down—that was me, and I knew it.

JOYCE: My mother begged us to talk to Jamie. She said, "She's your daughter; you need to talk to her."

JOHN: They didn't know the history. They didn't know how many years this had been going on. We told them only what we allowed ourselves to know; and, realistically, what we told them was probably only half of that. They knew only the tip of the iceberg. They never, ever knew about the iceberg.

JOYCE: We told them that Jamie had behavioral problems. She was explosive, she had been to therapy. She always had trouble with normal situations. She was volatile and all of our parents knew this about her. She was difficult to relate to because she had these emotional problems.

JOHN: That's how we continued to explain the situation. At that time, Jamie had not yet been diagnosed with attention-deficit disorder, her learning issues were not fully understood nor had her mood swings been diagnosed. Although we knew she had these difficulties, they had not been professionally diagnosed and treated with the proper medications. These problems were exacerbated by the alcohol issues.

JOYCE: In any case, we just couldn't do it. We couldn't talk to her. After the anger settled down, there was such a deep sense of sadness and loss, of pain, of regret and hopelessness, that we couldn't change anything. We were out of solutions.

JOHN: We were also out of energy.

JOYCE: The only energy I was getting was from my anger and, of course, that was not sustainable.

JAMIE: I think you told me I couldn't come home, didn't you? And that's why I moved back to Myrtle Beach.

JOYCE: We just needed some time to pass. We were so very, very angry with you.

JAMIE: I remember being glad the car was gone. It was the car I was raped on. For me, there was something positive in that, as sick as that may sound.

JOYCE: I thought, "Couldn't you have just traded it in?"

Bad Boyfriends

JOYCE: The next thing I knew, Jamie was on the phone, telling us about her boyfriend back in Myrtle Beach. It was her former manager, the guy we met at the dinner after the rape. He was the one who thought it was okay that she was drinking the next day. Jamie had a question for me. She wanted to know what love felt like. She thought these were the feelings she was having. She missed this guy. Maybe, she thought, she was in love.

JAMIE: I was so thrilled. I was always like this hopeless romantic. It was always my dream to get married. Every time I met someone, I thought about marrying him. I had all sorts of delusions about what it would be like.

JOYCE: Full of this newfound love, Jamie decided to move out of my parents' apartment, back to Myrtle Beach, to be with her new old boyfriend. It was the Christmas season and we had flown down to Florida to spend the holidays with our parents. Jamie must have thought it would be a good time to make yet another move, to escape from her situation. I know it was a relief to my parents, who were so worried about her. They couldn't deal with the responsibility and the pain of seeing what was happening. They must have felt the same sense of relief and hope we often felt when Jamie embarked on a new life plan. Together, we helped pack up all her things. We loaded them into a U-Haul behind the boyfriend's truck, and off she went with Mr. It's all good.

JAMIE: I was 27. This man was a 43-year-old Virginian whose mantra was, "It's all good, baby."

JOHN: She may have been 27, but she was acting like a 14-year-old. All of us at some points in our lives live in that past-present time. This was especially true for Jamie at this time. She had started drinking when she was 14. In many ways, she stopped developing emotionally and socially at that age.

JOYCE: Once again, John and I said to each other, "He's older, he has a job, and maybe he'll take care of her. Maybe he'll protect her. He seems to really love her. Maybe she will get married."

JOHN: In early February, we went to Myrtle Beach to visit them. They lived in a trailer. I remember walking around the trailer, thinking she must feel really closed in. I say this because of the rape. When it appears as though there is no room to escape, anxiety and panic can set in. That's how the trailer park felt and that's how her relationship with this man appeared to me to be. He controlled her.

JOYCE: Even though the place was tiny, Jamie seemed to feel comfortable there. There was a dartboard in the trailer. Jamie was very, very good at playing darts. The story they spun for us was that the purpose of the dartboard was so that Jamie could play this game she loved at home instead of going to a bar. Still, I didn't see her drinking, but she wasn't looking very good.

JAMIE: That's because we were doing coke again. My new guy was doing coke regularly. I was living in a trailer with him. He was now a manager of a strip club. I was staying home every day, smoking joints, drinking and doing coke at night, numbing. I was numbing the rape, the DWI, my feelings, anyone else's feelings—numbing whatever made me feel.

JOHN: And we really didn't see anything odd. She didn't do drugs or drink in front of us, and by that time, we wouldn't have recognized it if she were.

Painful Passages

JOHN: We weren't even home a week when we got a call from my mom. My father's condition had taken a turn for the worse; he was deteriorating rapidly.

My dad's cancer was taking a toll on my mom. After a long battle, he finally agreed to home hospice care. I received a call from my mom indicating that she needed some help. I decided to be with them both during this time. I flew down to make arrangements for home care, as Dad would not go to a hospital. I knew my mom was relieved and I flew back home thinking that things were under control. In my next conversation with my mom, she admitted that as soon as I had left the house, my dad made her cancel the hospice arrangements.

I had conflicted feelings. At first I was angry that once again he was so self-absorbed that he couldn't think of the toll taking care of him was taking on my mother. Then I would realize he was dying, and he probably had no idea what that meant to anyone else.

Within a month, Mom called again. This time I arranged for hospice care over the phone and Mom agreed to accept it. I guess by that time my dad was just too sick to fight. When the call came that he was within days of passing, I flew down once again. Since Dad knew I was the one who had insisted on hospice care, he did not greet me too warmly. When I walked in the door, my mom said, "John's here," and he said, "So what?" I knew then that this was not to be an easy good-bye.

To be with one's parent during his time of passing is different for every person. For me, regardless of his alcohol history, I felt honored to be at his side as he exhaled from this earth and inhaled in eternity. I felt as though I were standing between the worlds, acting as a bridge for him to cross. None of the words that could not be said during our lifetime together were important now. He was my father and he had done the best he could. That's all any of us can do. Ten years later, as I am writing this passage, I find tears welling up in my eyes, asking his forgiveness for my high expectations of him. That was not important when I was young and it was incomprehensible when I was a kid living in an alcoholic home. However, being older now, I do understand and know from my heart that he did do the best he could.

During the wake, the family came and told stories. Every story was about the times my dad and other family members drank. When we went back to the house after the wake, I poured my aunt a drink of vodka. She reproached me by indicating quite clearly, "I asked for a drink, not a drop." That's how it always seemed. As we were cleaning up after the extended family went home, I found bottles in the file cabinets in the garage and even one in the flowerpot on the front porch. My dad always told my mom he was going to work in the garage or take out the garbage. She thought that was so good of him. It was. But I doubt that she wanted to know about the extracurricular activity that accompanied his chores.

So what went unsaid stayed unsaid, even after he died.

I hate to admit this, but after his death and prior to my returning home, I felt a sense of relief. Even as I write this, I feel somewhat guilty about saying it, as I think I am betraying my dad. He had such a control over my mom; yet she seemed so grateful for any little thing he "allowed" her to buy. I knew how much she loved palm trees. Immediately after his death, Joyce and I went to a nursery and ordered a beautiful palm tree, along with some assorted shrubs that made the house look so inviting and cheery. It was almost a celebration. The reign of suppression to which alcohol contributes in many ways was over. It was a shame that my dad's passing rather than his sobriety helped plant the palm tree.

JOYCE: Henrietta, John's mother, put off dealing with her own illness until after his father was gone. By then, her cancer had begun to spread. The doctor said she needed chemotherapy, but she was having a difficult time with the idea of being sick and facing that without her husband.

JOHN: My mother didn't want to have the chemo treatments, but we convinced her that she should. She was strong and had so much to live for. She agreed to take the treatments. She had a severe toxic reaction to the first dose. Two days later, we got a call from my uncle telling us she was hospitalized. We were so alarmed that we got onto a plane the next morning and flew down to Florida. When we got to the hospital that evening, we were shocked to see her in such a terrible condition. She was semiconscious, but she seemed to be trying to say she wanted us to take her home.

JOYCE: Her condition seemed critical. We weren't sure she was going to make it. We were so shocked that we questioned the doctor about how this could have happened in just one day. He told us that she was just dehydrated and that we would see a great improvement in the morning. Again, I thought I must have been overreacting, as usual. So at 10 p.m. we went back to her house to unpack our things. Just before 11 p.m., we got a call from the hospital. Henrietta was dying.

JOHN: We ran to the car and sped back to the hospital, but when we arrived, she was already gone. It was a terrible thing. It all happened in one day. Less than 24 hours from the first call, there we were, walking out of the hospital with this little bag of her belongings.

JOYCE: It was so hard to comprehend. Just two days before, she was telling us about how funny her favorite TV program was. Now she was gone. How could that doctor not have known how close to death she was?

Jamie was very close to John's mom, and I knew this loss would be devastating to her. She knew we were at the hospital, but now I had to tell her Henrietta was gone.

I never expected her reaction. I couldn't believe it. Jamie started carrying on about her problems—about her boyfriend, about her life. It sounded like nonsense to me. Our hearts were broken. This woman whom we loved so deeply had just died, and Jamie was so self-consumed that she couldn't stop ranting long enough to feel the loss or hear our pain. I was furious with Jamie. I said, "Your father's heart is broken. My heart is broken. Your grandmother has just died. I don't have any energy to give you right now, Jamie. You are not the center of the universe right now." I told her to get down to Florida and I hung up.

We didn't hear from her for another day.

JAMIE: That's because my boyfriend had pulled out the phone lines. About that time, he started becoming abusive and he'd lock me out of the trailer. The night I found out that my grandmother had died, he smacked me. And he was a big guy. After he hit me, he left the trailer and I started to pack up to go to Florida. It was a nightmare trying to get away from him. I had to have the police come and watch me pack my stuff so that he wouldn't get abusive.

JOHN: The Beast, once again, prevented her from being with us when I needed her to be there.

My mother was undoubtedly one of the most unconditionally loving people I had ever known. She adored Jamie. I wanted our whole family to be there with her when she passed. It was not meant to be. I so much desired to be with her during her transition. It just did not happen that way. I felt so supported by Joyce as she walked side by side with me and simultaneously so heartsick that my daughter, who was cherished by my mother and who cherished her in return, could not be there with us at that time.

There were two distinct realities occurring simultaneously with Jamie, Joyce and me. I knew only that Jamie was not there at such an important time and I did not know that her boyfriend was beating her up at the time we were trying to get hold of her. This is what the program means when it says if the drugs don't kill you, the lifestyle will. Gradually, but most assuredly, it takes away pieces of your life. It keeps you from being present for the most precious moments of life.

JAMIE: During all of this, everything was caving in on me. Here I was, clearly addicted, in an abusive relationship and getting kicked out of even that. I couldn't go back to my parents. I couldn't go to my grandparents. I couldn't go home.

When he pulled the phone wires out, I was pissed. I didn't even have a cell phone. It was only when a friend came over with a cell phone that I could call my parents back. Of course, I was devastated, I was sad, I was worried; I was hurting, too. And, of course, I was broke. Mom was so mad at me. She basically had to walk me through how to get on the plane, because I didn't have any money and I didn't know what to do. And I showed up with bruises on my arms.

JOHN: I wasn't in a position to hear about it, nor did I want to.

JAMIE: The reality of Grandma's death really hit me when I saw my family. I was going through extreme loss, heartache, desperation, pain. But I didn't want to tell anyone. Anger was always my outward emotion, the secondary emotion. The underlying feelings were hurt, disappointment in myself and knowing I disappointed everyone else. Again.

JOYCE: And expressing none of it verbally.

JAMIE: I was crying all the time.

JOYCE: But she didn't talk.

JAMIE: My cousins were there. I talked to them a lot about what was going on with me, what happened with Mr. It's all good.

JOYCE: I knew she was upset, but I wasn't sure what had happened and I didn't ask. There was too much going on. I didn't want to focus on Jamie. I didn't have any more energy for her.

JAMIE: We were all focused on my grieving for my grandmother.

JOYCE: I do remember the boyfriend's calling more than once and wanting to come to the funeral. We didn't know he had been hitting her, but we certainly didn't want him to come, which she was happy with.

JOHN: There was something that happened as we were packing up that was later to become significant.

JAMIE: We were going through my grandmother's belongings. There were four of us—myself and my three female cousins—and we got to Grandma's jewelry. When we got to the wedding band, they all said that I could have it. All of them had been married and had their own wedding rings, so they agreed the ring should go to me.

JOYCE: Henrietta didn't have much, but there was this beautiful delicate wedding ring. It was so sweet, the cousins' telling Jamie that she could have it.

She put it on her finger and everyone cried.

More Good-byes and a New Threat

JAMIE: I moved back to Myrtle Beach and stayed with a friend and her mother. It was then that the panic attacks really started to kick in. I was getting them more frequently. I was having drenching night sweats. I felt like I was going to die when it was happening. I felt like someone was choking me. I would be very disoriented. I wouldn't realize where I was. I was paranoid. I closed all the blinds in the room, I locked the doors; I wouldn't let anyone come near me.

JOYCE: Two weeks after Henrietta died, her sister, who was her best friend, died. They always had been like twins. We had spent a lot of time with Aunt Loretta, and John had spent all his summers at her country home in Port Jervis. On the way out of the parking lot at

Aunt Loretta's funeral, John mentioned that he had blood in his urine. Two weeks later, he was diagnosed with bladder cancer and within a month, he had his first surgery.

Then we got a letter from Jamie:

May 29, 1999

I really don't know where to begin, seeing as how I haven't written for so long. . . . I need to find out what I want and where I want to be. I wasn't planning on falling in love, which I did, and am so torn.

The letter wasn't signed. She was now with a different guy.

JAMIE: He was another drug dealer. There wasn't anything violent or abusive with him. He was just another guy who could help me not feel.

JOYCE: John wrote back to her. He had just spoken with her on the phone about this guy and wanted to give her some advice.

Father's Day Evening
Dear Jamie,

Just got off the phone with you and heard your level of difficulties. One thing that has really helped me when I saw or see things that are always negative is this: I ask myself what is this reflection to me in my own life, particularly about what I may be thinking about myself. Am I this negative to myself? Usually when people always find fault or fail to see the good or recognize the good in life or themselves they are projecting. In other words, they don't see the good in themselves—or they consider that they are not enough.

I would ask that you consider that question yourself. Are you saying that about yourself? God places us in contact with others so they can mirror our true perfection or our blind spots of our own personalities. Assume you have placed yourself in the right place and your great need to see the people differently. They may only be mirroring to you how negative you can be toward yourself so you can see it, stop it and allow God to change it for you.

Use this time for yourself. Your good friends and we will be here for you with open arms when you are truly ready to return. Trust yourself and your decisions. We love you so very much.

Take care—continue to write—stay in touch.

Love,

Us

That was on Father's Day.

JAMIE: I'm an addict. I will use anything that will take me outside myself. Men did that for me. I didn't have to think about myself when I was with a guy. I spent all my time thinking about him, our relationship, what would happen in our future. When I was with a guy, I never had to think about what was really going on.

JOYCE: I remember her telling us he was her soul mate.

JAMIE: They were all my soul mates. He would have been a really good guy if he weren't a drug addict. He would cut lines of coke that were like road maps—they were big. I was doing so much coke, though, that I was developing a huge tolerance. It also changed from just getting high so I could cover up my feelings to really liking the high. I started to get the euphoric thing going. And we were using every night. It came out of his supply. I didn't have to pay for anything, ever.

During the day, I wasn't doing anything—we slept. When we got up, I'd move my clothes around, do nothing. We spent all day coming down from the high of the night before.

JOYCE: We had a feeling that something shifted but didn't know exactly what it was. We suspected that she was doing drugs, but we did not know how much.

JAMIE: We ate every night, right before we got high. While this was going on, Dad was sick. I was paying attention, but it wasn't really until he was going to have the second surgery that the importance of it hit me. All of a sudden, I got how serious it was, how sick Dad was. My feelings were beginning to leave me even when I was not using. So I packed up and moved back home with my parents the day before Dad had the second surgery.

JOHN: I was happy that Jamie was coming home. I was always glad that she was there, that she was safe. But I was in a state of shock at that time. Within a few weeks, my mother had died, my aunt had died and I was diagnosed with cancer. I called it "baby cancer," trying to minimize it.

JOYCE: He was in denial!

JOHN: I had two surgeries in three months. I wasn't really paying attention to Jamie's problems. I felt that her new boyfriend was more important to her than my being in the hospital.

JOYCE: Jamie had gone out the night before the surgery and I had to wake her up. She said, "I don't like going to hospitals; it reminds me of the rape."

I said, "I don't give a f..., we're going to the hospital." She was getting quite self-righteous. She was always being put out.

JOHN: Joyce was always there for me. She always stood up for me. I could always count on her, where I knew that I could not count on Jamie at all.

JAMIE: I think my behavior was a defense mechanism. I didn't want to have to see my dad and feel something. I thought that if I felt one thing, I would have to feel all of them. The only feeling I liked was being high.

JOHN: I didn't know that you didn't want to go because you didn't want to have to see me and feel something. I guess I didn't want to feel how bad I felt that you were not there for me when I was in the hospital. I couldn't. I so wished you had been able to be there for your mom and me during that time. I believe that's what families are supposed to be about. You saw us do it when my dad had cancer. I did it because I loved him. I thought, "Where is my daughter?" I didn't want to say anything to Joyce, because I knew it would get her more upset when she saw how upset I was. I didn't want her to feel any more pain or helplessness than what she was feeling already. On some level, I also knew Jamie could just not do this. So it wasn't judgment as much as resignation. However, my resignation was not acceptance. There was no peace. I ached. My mother's death, my aunt's death (she being a second mother to me), Jamie's rape, ongoing drinking and drugging, and now cancer, was just a bit too much to deal with.

I decided to go with my old friend denial: Let's pretend it's not as bad as I think it is. It will help me get through.

JOYCE: All I could see was that there was no compassion. At that time, I was continuously furious with her, but never *to* her. I was still afraid of her fragility, afraid that if I got mad at her, it would hurt her. The fragility was, to me, becoming an issue of mental illness. She wasn't doing anything for herself. She wasn't talking, she wasn't expressing; but everything was about Jamie, as usual.

JAMIE: I don't think I had any idea of how furious my parents were. When Mom talks about the fragility, she's right. I was literally on the brink of insanity. I was going right down the list of things that full-blown addicts do. I lost the ability to deal with anything. I copped, not coped. I couldn't cope with a napkin's not being folded right; how could I cope with reality?

JOYCE: John rarely expressed his anger. He was still pretty much in denial, and now he was sick. So I really couldn't do anything except take care of him. I needed to take care of my sick daughter. I needed to take care of my sick parents and I needed to be competent for a very demanding job at the Department of Health.

I found comfort in viewing my situation from a metaphysical point of view. I had been going to a metaphysical church and attending spiritual retreats for more than a decade. I would meditate, pray and find comfort in my deeply rooted spiritual beliefs. At this point, our friends were saying, "It's time Jamie stood up for herself; it's time you stopped supporting her." They were becoming adamant about her taking advantage of our hospitality.

I'd think, "Well, they are right. It's long past time for her to be independent."

And then I'd look at her. She was forsaken. She weighed about 90 pounds; she was shaking all the time. It was impossible for me to do what they said I should. I could not turn her out.

JOHN: One of the things we did to cope was to see, as much as possible, the spiritual being Jamie was that went beyond the addiction.

JOYCE: Until that point, though, we always tried to "fix" Jamie, fix her life. But that just wasn't working.

JOHN: So we made a conscious decision to do what we could, and that was to focus on Jamie's well-being and not on Jamie's story. That story was an endless engagement with horror. We couldn't do anything to change it, but we could help her remember who she really was. We felt we could do that by holding the true memory of her until she was ready to receive it. That required us to allow life to be, which is incredibly freeing, though, on the face of it, it was intolerably fearful.

We made up our own story. This beautiful, spiritual being, who was our daughter, was going through a process that she chose. Joyce and I began to have many discussions about holding her in the light of creation. We focused on how much we loved her and not on her present situations. This love became a love of allowing and not a love of urgency. Just because she decided to live in hell did not mean we had to be there with her. It was a tremendous decision for us—a commitment to ourselves.

This decision became a practice, not an instant cure. Every day there would be a situation that would startle us emotionally. It would require us to rest in stillness—to be soothed by the loving forces of the universe. We would breathe and take in life and allow life to take us in. Two gifts received from the recovery process began to unfold for us at this time: to learn to love unconditionally and experience the relief that brings and to allow ourselves to be supported by life beyond our understanding of it in the present.

The principles I had embraced when I returned home from the retreat were also extremely beneficial to me at that time. If nothing outside myself can either make me whole or take away from the wholeness I already am, then Jamie's sobriety is no longer a condition of my internal peace.

If I no longer need to rely solely on myself, I can ask for support from this impersonal, yet very personal, universe to touch my brokenness and heal me when I find it hard to believe that nothing outside myself can disturb my peace.

There are no exceptions to the idea that we are innocent beyond our wildest dreams. Therefore, it became easier for me not to judge myself, Joyce or Jamie. None of us was waking up in the morning with an expressed intent to do harm to another. We were doing the best we could with all we had. Last, and probably the most difficult to explain, was that I began to understand that behind Jamie's addiction was the even deeper lesson.

What if her addiction were not a singular isolated event occurring separately within a family unit? If all of us are cocreators of the universe, what was my part in this creation of madness? What if one of the purposes of Jamie's addiction were to free me? What if I were loved so much by her that she took on a disability and lived it in order to relieve me of my own prison of conditional loving of myself and others? What if her addiction were here to teach me to create space, time and opportunity for myself, even in the light of another's misery? What if her addiction were here to teach me that no matter how much love we have for another, the other has to say yes to that love? Love can never be forced upon another.

When I began to see the addiction in this light, I realized how important it was to heal myself so that I no longer unconsciously needed her addiction to set me free or keep me in my own prison. Once my intent was to be at peace, I cut the connection that I had to have her continue to be addicted. She was then free to decide to continue to be active or be relieved of her unconscious desire to free me. Until I accepted my own healing in its totality, I would still be contributing to the need for Jamie to carry on with her addiction.

JOYCE: We believed in the healing power of prayer and meditation, and I think that belief was the single most important thing that helped us keep our sanity, or at least believe we were sane.

EIGHT

. . . .

Crashing at High Speed

JOYCE: This is probably a very good example of distorted, codependent thinking. We knew it was important for all of us that Jamie move out of our house. She needed to live on her own. So here comes the wishful thinking: We thought that if Jamie had something of her own, she'd be more responsible. We didn't want her living in our house, because she was unwilling to consider the impact of her late hours on our well-being. Her presence on a daily basis was too painful. So we bought a condo in the next town, figuring that Jamie could get a roommate and pay rent to us rather than to someone else. Eventually, she would be able to save enough and own the condo. We would all win. We saw it as an investment.

JOHN: We couldn't live with her anymore.

JAMIE: It seemed like a good idea to me as well, at least to the part of me that could still think straight. I started working at a towing and transport company as an associate auction co-coordinator. I would go to car auctions and arrange for transport of cars on behalf of dealerships. It paid $11.50 an hour.

JOHN: For a brief moment, we saw Jamie as she really was, the person beyond the addiction. She was smart, capable and responsible.

JAMIE: I was doing all right in my day job, but I was also bartending again
on the weekends. I met W at the bar. He owned his own pool company
and made really good money. We hooked up. He needed a place to
stay, so we moved in together. It was a platonic relationship. He was
also a drinker.

JOYCE: We had no idea he was a drinker. It looked to us that she was on the
right path—again. W was a good guy. He had money. He worked hard.
It was a platonic relationship, as Jamie said. He was going to have an
arranged marriage in Korea. We took that to mean he held traditional
values. So we took a breath and said, "Finally, things are changing."

JAMIE: But they weren't. One Friday, when I wasn't working, I got drunk
and got another DWI.

JOYCE: I didn't know about that until now. Thank God I didn't.

JAMIE: W bailed me out. We went home to the condo and W said, "Let's
party." So we did. When the guys at the towing company found out,
they said that I could have called them and they would have bailed me
out. Guys were always willing to help. Getting in trouble was one way
I had their attention.

The towing company eventually went bankrupt, though, and the
business shut down. That's when I got my next day-care job. I was
the head teacher for a day-care center. I worked there for a while.

JOYCE: Her behavior was very similar to John's father's. She could do all
this drinking and drugging and still show up for work. No one would
know. She was a master at lying and manipulating and putting on a
good face.

JOHN: The fact is, she always worked. She had been working since she was 14 years old. She could show up for work but not for life.

JAMIE: One night I was out at a bar and I was looking for coke. I met a guy who said he could get me some. We went to Troy and met this girl. It ended up that she had crack, not coke. She said she wouldn't give it to me, because she wouldn't do that to anyone. She knew I'd get addicted. But the guy was willing to give it to me. So we all used that night. It was my first experience with crack. And after we smoked, we went to a bar and had a few drinks.

About a week later, I called this girl and we became friends and started using crack regularly. I found out that W used as well; he just never did it at home. So he and I started doing it together.

JOYCE: How does that happen? How do you even have that conversation? "Hi, you don't know me, but I want to know if you can get me some crack." How do you do that?

JAMIE: How does it not happen? Bars are the easiest places to get drugs; so are the streets. Addicts do not have to look very hard to find drugs. We can sniff them out like canines. For someone who is not an addict, this may seem strange, but for someone who is, no explanation is needed. Between W and my girlfriend, I was well supplied with crack on a regular basis. At the same time, I was seeing a therapist for the panic attacks. She prescribed an anti-anxiety drug.

JOYCE: I felt that this therapist was minimizing Jamie's drinking problem. She just had anxiety problems was what they would say. Hello!

JAMIE: That's because I was lying to the therapist, as I lied to everyone. I was a manipulator, like all addicts.

JOYCE: Then an new guy appeared.

JAMIE: G worked at the towing company. He was a real jerk. He wasn't really an alcoholic. He drank, but not in excess. But he did do coke. One night I went out with him to shoot pool. We had gotten some coke. We ended up getting in a fight in the car outside the pool hall. My high heel got caught in the door as he pushed me out of the truck and I broke my ankle.

The police came that night and they were laughing. I was so angry with them. They were laughing at me because I was being so melodramatic: "He did this to me, he did that, he's a jerk"—I was going on and on. When they left, I went out and got high on crack. Then I went back home and took the bottle of pills the therapist had given me. I didn't really want to die; I just wanted to stop using and hurting and being in pain. After I took the pills, I called a friend and told her what I had done. I also called another guy I got high with. He came and drove me to the hospital.

JOYCE: The next afternoon, Jamie's friend called us and said Jamie was in the hospital. She had broken her ankle. No one told us anything about the overdose.

JOHN: Her story was that G had pushed her out of the truck. She didn't want to talk to us. She was shocked and angry to see us at the hospital.

JOYCE: She didn't call us. She wasn't going to tell us anything. So when we showed up, she was shocked, and she wouldn't even look at us.

JOHN: Jamie had already been discharged when we arrived. She was being wheeled out of the hospital. A friend went to the hospital with us. We told her that Jamie had broken her ankle and it was G's fault. She'd been with us through all of these episodes, so she went along to lend us moral support. Now our friends were getting involved in the rescue efforts; but they were not seeing it the same way we were.

JAMIE: They didn't know I was smoking crack.

JOYCE: We still didn't know for sure she was doing drugs at all.

JAMIE: When I was leaving the hospital, my parents came rushing in. They told me they loved me. The more they told me they loved me, the more I hurt, because I knew I didn't deserve to be loved. I certainly didn't love me; how could they? I thought, "If they only knew everything."

JOHN: The next days were horrible. We could see how sick Jamie was. We couldn't ignore or deny it any longer. Joyce and I were desperate. We decided to confront Jamie and insist that she get treatment. Besides, after the pill incident—the attempted suicide—the medical authorities were legally bound to mandate outpatient care.

JOYCE: On May 9, 2000, we went to a clinical-services outpatient evaluation center. The first thing they do is assess the situation to determine the level of care needed.

JAMIE: They gave me a series of questions. They asked things such as "Have you ever broken a bone?" " Have you ever had a blackout?" "Have you ever had a DWI?" The only question I said no to was "Do you ever drink in the morning?"

JOHN: She didn't lie to them this time. She knew, at some level, that she needed help. For me, it was a great day. I felt a sense of relief. For the first time, the three of us together were going to tackle the problem. We were relieved that there were now addiction-treatment people involved.

JOYCE: Yeah, it was a great day. No one died.

JAMIE: The care they recommended was intensive outpatient treatment.

JOYCE: That was another feeling of relief for us. If they didn't think she had to go to an inpatient program, maybe she wasn't in as bad a condition as we imagined. How could she be if they weren't going to admit her to a 28-day inpatient program? Maybe I was overreacting, after all.

Here again, the disease wreaked havoc with my emotions. On the one hand, I felt so relieved that professionals were saying that Jamie wasn't sick enough to require inpatient treatment. On the other hand, I feared that outpatient support was not enough to face down The Beast.

JOHN: I was hoping they would admit her to the inpatient program; but this was better than nothing.

JOYCE: We met with the staff after they gave the recommendation. I remember wanting to make sure they knew everything that had happened. We told them everything. Since Jamie started drinking in high school, I had been concerned that no one else saw what I did. I was always trying to get other people to see what I saw.

JOHN: So we didn't leave anything out. Later we learned that to be admitted to an inpatient program, there are specific requirements.

JOYCE: The next day, I went to Long Island to help my parents move back into their summer camp. We spent the day at doctors' appointments and I signed my mother up for hospice. She was furious with me. I tried to convince her that it was a way to get both of them some assistance with taking care of their medical needs. She said it meant she was going to die. She looked at me as though I had given her a death sentence.

I thought my heart was going to break as I tried to be strong and compassionate while all I wanted to do was to cry for my beautiful parents and for myself. I tried to comprehend how my vital, competent, strong parents had become so frail. It was late in the evening when I finally got them settled into the house. My dad was relieved that Mom would be having a nurse come in; he needed one, too. He had spent the day on dialysis for his heart failure and they told me his condition was critical. Still, he had bounced back from serious threats before. We tried to line up his 32 pills and figure out the doses. He was tired, he said, and needed to get to bed. He turned to me and reminded me that I had to call the cable company in the morning. He needed to see the basketball play-offs. He walked down the hall and I went to make a cup of tea for Mom. There came a loud thump from the bedroom. I called out, but Dad didn't answer. He had fallen and was obviously not breathing. I ran to him and tried to resuscitate him. As I was holding his head, I looked up and saw him standing over his body. He reached his hand out and suddenly I remembered. I said, "Oh, you want me to walk you over?" I saw him smile and suddenly I was there on the floor again, grabbing the phone and calling 911. But of course I knew he was gone. My mother stood in the room and didn't speak a word. She went into shock and shut down.

All day we had been reminiscing, because it was their 54th wedding anniversary, and now he was gone.

JOHN: Jamie and I drove down to Long Island the next day. It had been only a few days since she had entered a treatment program. During the entire trip to Long Island, Jamie was on the phone talking to her support people about her problems. It was constant. There was very little outward recognition of others around her at that point and what they might be experiencing. On some level, I certainly understood the importance of her keeping contact with people in the program. It was critical for her sobriety, as she was so fragile at the time and she loved her grandfather so much, and I so wished she could have been present to support her mom. It was another moment when parents wish their kid could stand by them during a crucial loss in their life. We were so involved in our own grief that there was no space to recognize the intent of Jamie's actions to remain sober and drug free for this loss in her life. So much was happening with each of us at the same time. I was trying to be present for Joyce, be supportive of Jamie and feel my own feelings for this man I loved as deeply as my own father.

This is such a clear demonstration of the wisdom of the recovery program's strongly advising people not to get involved in relationships for at least one year after stopping using or drinking. The need to focus on your recovery is paramount and it can be very difficult to be available for another's situation while struggling to be clean. Even though the person in recovery wants to be present, he or she may not be able to show it, and this can cause major resentment.

JOYCE: When they arrived, Jamie was a real mess. She was having panic attacks. She kept shaking and chain smoking outside the funeral parlor. She hobbled around on crutches, looking like an escapee from an institution. My family looked at her and asked us, "What's wrong with Jamie?"

JOHN: What could we say to them without sitting them down for two days and giving them the whole story?

JOYCE: It was horrible. My beloved dad had just died. My mother was in shock. John had just come through the cancer. Jamie was barely alive. I remember thinking to myself, "The four closest people to me are either dead or dying."

The day my dad died, I knew something was going on. I got up at five a.m., which I never did. I'm not a morning person. I wrote my parents a letter about how much I loved them. We had the day with one another and we talked about their 54 years together. I was grateful for the fact that my dad had given me the honor of helping him cross over. I stayed in that place of gratefulness for a whole week until my brother and I started fighting about our mother's care. For a short period, my focus had shifted from keeping Jamie alive to dealing with my parents' dying.

JAMIE: I remember feeling proud that I was clean for my grandfather's funeral. At the same time, it had been three days since I had had a drink or a hit and I was definitely feeling fuzzy and confused and depressed. When you get into recovery and experience a loss for the first time, you relive all the losses prior to the new loss. My grandfather's death again put me into psychological, emotional trauma.

I wasn't completely self-obsessed, though, even if it did look that way to my family. I was really worried about my grandmother, really, really worried. She wasn't talking. I don't think she even cried that much. She was like a stone, and it scared me. I didn't know how to deal with it. When she had found out she had cancer, she had just come apart, crying and sobbing. Now her husband had just died and there was nothing in her.

I was also worried about my mom. I loved my mom so much, despite the fact that I was an addict and an alcoholic. I began to think about what it would be like if she had been the one with cancer or dying. I was proud of myself, though, because, over the three days, we ate out a lot. When people would start drinking, I would leave the restaurant. I remember going back to my group at home and saying, "Look what I did: My grandfather died and I didn't drink. My family drank and I didn't." I was just new in recovery, but I was already starting to talk the language. I was going to make it!

JOHN: Some families have certain members of their tribe who just mean so much to everyone. That was my father-in-law. We nicknamed him Mr. PIA because he was such a pain in the ass, and yet so full of life. His life touched so many people and all of them had a special moment they remembered about their relationship with him.

Grace filled the room as we, as a family, were all present, damaged as we were. Nonetheless, we were together while honoring and burying this man who had brought such joy to our lives.

JOYCE: We returned home weary and trying to grasp the magnitude of the major events that were occurring so rapidly in our lives. Each morning we would wake early to meditate and pray before we began to face the day. One morning shortly after my father's death, I was disturbed from my meditation by a scratching on the window screen in the bedroom. I opened my eyes to see an American goldfinch staring through the window at me. Now, this was strange enough, since we lived in the wilderness. But it was to become even more profound. John came running up to the bedroom. He had been downstairs in his office doing his morning meditation when he was disturbed by a scratching on the screen. Yes, it was the same goldfinch. We looked at each other in amazement, because whenever my father came to visit, he would love to watch the goldfinches perching on the trees in the yard around the house. But he insisted they were wild canaries. We argued with him so many times, showing him Audubon photos of the bird called goldfinch. Still, he insisted they were wild canaries. Now this goldfinch was scratching on our window screen. The bird came every morning for quite some time. It looked into the room. It posed for photos. There was no doubt in my mind. My dad had come to tell us he was free and he would be there to help us if we needed him.

More Graduations

JOYCE: Three months later, Jamie graduated from the outpatient treatment program. We could breathe a sigh of relief and hope—couldn't we?

JOHN: As far as we knew, Jamie was clean the whole time, which really was quite an accomplishment.

JOYCE: We were convinced she was on her way.

JAMIE: I had to keep going to meetings. I had to find a sponsor. That is when they say the active addiction is gone and addicts have to deal with restructuring their lives, for real. I wanted to work a program. I wanted to get clean.

JOHN: The center was telling us that Jamie had done everything she needed to be successful. She had the support around her, she had made the decision. Now it was up to her to do it day by day. They were confident that she was going to be one of the addicts who made it.

JOYCE: My mother never returned to that house after my dad died. That very night, she moved in with my brother and they continued daily hospice care. Almost every weekend John and I drove the four hours to spend time with Mom and give my brother a break from her care.

JOHN: During this time, much of the family's attention was focused on the party being planned in New York City for the 50th wedding anniversary of Joyce's aunt (her mother's sister).

JOYCE: Staying alive for the party became a way for my mom to keep focused on a positive goal. She really wanted to be at the party. I bought her a new outfit and I tried to look happy, but I knew it would be the outfit that I would bury her in. A few days before the party, my brother called to say my mom had taken a turn for the worse and I should come down right away. While I was on the phone with him, there came the familiar scratching on the window screen. As we spoke, the goldfinch leaned its head on the screen and started to sing. It sang so loudly I could hardly hear what my brother was saying.

When I arrived on Long Island that afternoon, I found my mom weak and obviously struggling. She refused to go back to bed, so we sat on the sofa together all night. In the morning (the day before the party), with her head on my shoulder, she lost consciousness. Only a few moments later, her brother and his family arrived from California. They came in with my aunt and uncle, who were expecting Mom to be happy to see them. The plan was that this would help her find the energy to go to the party. But Mom was not conscious. We all started to cry. They asked what they should do; they were going to cancel the party. We were all in shock. Hospice was arriving to put my mom on a hospital bed in the den while we were convincing my aunt and uncle that it was all right to go ahead with the party. My mother had said she was worried that she was going to ruin the party. We couldn't let that happen. But my aunt insisted she would do it only if my brother and I were going to attend. So we did. My cousin Marge came to be with Jamie and my mother while we went to New York City for the party. Mom was still alive when we got home at one a.m. I sent everyone to bed and spent the rest of the night singing every song I knew to my mother so she would not be so afraid in her passage. At nine a.m., she took her last breath and I let go of her hand.

JAMIE: My grandmother really couldn't do anything on her own. Before she lost consciousness, I remember helping her in the washroom. She started to have a panic attack. I said, "Gram, just keep breathing." She was so scared. I said, "Gram, I have a lot of experience with this. I know."

She said, "Will you teach me?"

I was overwhelmed. I really felt a connectedness with her. When I'd use, I'd pray. I'd feel guilty when I'd get high, because I knew my grandparents were watching over me at some level. I always felt very connected with them.

Sharing the panic attacks with my grandmother was even more of a connection. It was like sitting in a room of addicts. They say there is nothing stronger than the therapeutic value of one addict helping another. For once, the roles were switched. I was the caretaker. It hadn't happened very often in my life. I was so glad I was sober for it.

JOYCE: My mom would allow Jamie to comfort her in ways she never did with me. I felt so thankful that Jamie was present for my mom. She had missed John's mother's death just the year before because she wasn't in recovery. But now she was here. She was sober. And she was witnessing what love asks of us and what it gives back. I felt so aware of the different forms that love takes and the power it has to heal. The universal sense of bonding and love that I was experiencing helped ease the pain of losing both of my parents within three months.

JOHN: Within a year, all four of our parents were gone, but we had our daughter back. Joyce and I held on to this loving feeling with everything we had.

NINE

Checking Out

JAMIE: I was still clean in August. But when I came back from Grandma's funeral, I picked up the crack again. I didn't drink, though.

JOYCE: We thought she was clean. We were feeling so confident, so proud, relieved—and hollow at the same time. So much had happened in two years. Our perspectives had shifted.

JAMIE: I was an addict. I was going to rationalize, justify and lie, and I'd believe the lies I told myself. I'd go to AA meetings and pick up a coin for X number of days of sobriety and tell them I was clean. In self-support groups we use coins to celebrate clean/sober dates. I was going to AA and saying I was sober because I wasn't drinking. I was using other substances, just not alcohol; therefore, in my mind, I was sober. But my addiction was progressing and progressing. I could never be a social crack smoker.

JOYCE: We didn't see much of her during that period. She was working at a day-care center and going to meetings.

JAMIE: The day-care job was okay. I always managed to show up for work. Dad had arranged to get me a job interview at a treatment center in Albany; but it required a drug test, so I didn't go to the interview.

JOYCE: She still wasn't looking good. We got into a big confrontation with her therapist. I kept saying, "She's still using. Look at her—she looks terrible." But the therapist defended her. Once again, I felt like I was the only one seeing it. Again, I was getting very fearful that I was making it up.

JAMIE: I was so thin at that time that my thighs didn't even touch. There was nothing in my refrigerator except water. I wasn't interested in eating. I was interested only in getting high.

JOYCE: Her therapist wasn't seeing any of this. She was fighting with me, telling me Jamie was not in jeopardy. And I was paying her to tell me that!

JAMIE: A crack high lasts ten minutes. You could do it and 15 minutes later no one would notice if, of course, they didn't know what the signs were. When you take a hit of crack, it automatically goes to the pleasure center of your brain, creating a state of euphoria. As soon as you come down, you want it again, which is why it becomes so dangerous. I'd go to my friend's house after work and smoke with her. But at one point, I started getting really, really neurotic and protective of my addiction. It got so that I didn't want to share with anyone. I just wanted to go home and do it myself.

One night, when I was at my friend's house, a drug dealer came in. He was a member of a gang. That didn't matter to me. All I was thinking about was how to get the stuff directly. He told us he lived ten minutes away from me. So I got his pager number. This is where things really started getting dangerous in a different way. I started meeting the dealers alone. I got to know them really well, because I was getting high every day.

I was spending all my paychecks real fast. Each one got me three or four hours of high. But, of course, that wasn't enough. I needed much more money. I got the bright idea that I would get my dad's checks, make them out, forge them and then take them to a place I used to work to cash them. I told the guy there that I was doing great, I wasn't drinking and life was good, and he would cash the checks for me. I had been taking money, too, for a long time, right out of my mom's wallet.

JOYCE: You know, it almost feels good to hear Jamie admit this. I used to think I was going crazy. I knew that I had a certain amount of money in my wallet. When I'd go to buy something, I'd notice 20 or 50 or 80 dollars would be missing.

I'd come home and tell John that money was missing from my wallet again. It was one more situation where Jamie's actions really affected our relationship. Here's how the conversation often went:

> *Me:* "I know I'm missing money from my wallet. I think Jamie is taking it."
>
> *John:* "Well, you shouldn't leave your money around where it can be taken."
>
> *Me:* "I'm not leaving it, for god's sake. It's in my friggin' wallet!"
>
> *John:* "Well, I'm just saying. . . ."

JOHN: Here I was again, adjusting to the situation. Rather than saying to Jamie, "You need to leave," I said to Joyce, "Don't leave your money where she can take it." It's a past-present response to my own lack of empowerment with my father's alcoholism. I am not defending it as much as pointing out how deeply our learned patterns of behavior are embedded in our brain.

JOYCE: This would make me furious. I took this to mean it was my problem. I should have been sleeping with my pocketbook under my pillow, just in case it was tempting someone to steal. No problem!

JAMIE: The reality was that this stealing started way back when I was 18.

JOYCE: I knew it at the time. I tried to confront her. I'd rant and rave about it. She always seemed to win the argument. She'd just lie her way out of it. She'd confuse and frustrate the hell out of me till I was exhausted from the fighting and the suspicion. I was so sad and angry about it. I think I still am.

JAMIE: My dad gave me a gas-station credit card. I'd put one dollar of gas on it and then fill up with beer.

JOHN: I saw that every now and then on the statements. But I don't remember seeing one dollar for gas and the rest for beer. The statements never said beer on them.

As I'm writing this section, I have a tremendous urge to explain my actions. I'm thinking that you, the reader, must be thinking, "What's wrong with this guy? Money is being stolen from his wife. His checks are being taken and not all the purchases on the credit card were for gas. Is he blind?"

Well, if I'm totally honest, I have to say I guess I was. On the other hand, the checks that were stolen from me were from a checkbook that I used only for taxes. I would put money in there but never use the checkbook to write checks, because it was a forced savings. I had little immediate occasion to suspect anything. The life of a family with an addict gets so crazy; you have a tendency to question your own judgment about what is real. And, again, to think my own daughter was stealing from me was so unfathomable; it was more palatable to ignore it. Sometimes things just cannot be digested at the time they are happening. It can be just too much.

JOYCE: This is a great example of the conversation we had for 20 years. No, she didn't misuse the card every time. He's right; she didn't do it every time. The point is that every time she would do something like this, I'd say, "Look at what she's doing. Don't you see what's happening?"

And he'd say, "Well, maybe she did that now, but she didn't do it every time." When he said that, it would make me furious. I'd end up screaming out of frustration and a desire to make him see what I saw. I would end up looking like a lunatic and he would say, "Calm down." He'd tell me I was overreacting. Immediately, the argument was between us, not about Jamie. I ended up not as the victim of the theft but as the out-of-control screamer who was always blowing things out of proportion. All the anger that should have been focused on Jamie's outrageous behavior was now sitting in the middle of our relationship.

JOHN: I don't like generalizations.

JOYCE: We could never get beyond that conversation, because it would stop right there. I'd get furious and we'd start yelling at each other. Until now, we never got beyond the details of what we were arguing about. We never really got to the point.

That is what was going without saying.

JOHN: It was so very difficult to believe that my daughter would steal from me that I would do absolutely anything to convince myself otherwise. There was a lesson in this for me. Although I knew it was important to hold her in my mind and heart in the highest possibility of herself to remind her who she really was, it was equally important to notice and respect the person of the person she thought herself to be at that time. She could not act out of her highest self, because she was trapped in this other way of being. Again, love can heal, but a person has to say yes to the healing. Jamie was not yet saying a full yes to this healing.

JOYCE: When I finally went through my checkbook, I realized that Jamie had been taking checks out of my checkbook as well. She would take them from the center or toward the end of the book, so that I wouldn't notice. It seemed unbelievable.

When I finally had to come to grips with the reality of it, I went to the bank and told them that my daughter was taking my checks. Then I heard myself saying she was an addict. I told them to arrest her if she showed up trying to cash a check with my name. I stood there crying, not believing that I was doing that.

JOHN: It was another horrible moment.

JOYCE: I thought my heart would break. The bank was in the building where I worked. I was on one side of the glass, sobbing, talking to a teller. It was the first time I said, "My daughter is an addict."

I went home and confronted Jamie. She said, "It wasn't me; I'd never do that to you."

I said, "Well, that's good, because the person who has been taking my checks is going to be arrested the next time he or she goes to the bank with one."

JAMIE: When my mother confronted me, I said, "Good; I hope they get them." I couldn't believe I was saying it. I was like a deer in the headlights. But, at that point, I was so wrapped up in my addiction that my thought was how to get out of this one but still keep getting high. In the meantime, my friend R called me up and said, "Jamie, you're in big trouble." The guy who had been cashing the checks found out that I had forged them and he was going to call the police. R stopped him and told me she was going to call my dad.

JOYCE: John still wasn't ready to believe Jamie would take our money. It took someone else to tell him. But now we realized that Jamie was still using.

Who's in Denial Now?

JOYCE: We moved into our house in Troy in April 2001 after a year of renovations. I often wondered why Jamie didn't come and help us. I was working so hard, and we were both so tired. When we finally were moving in, I really needed her help with unpacking. I still had all of our parents' things stored in unopened boxes. But Jamie would stop by only to check in and run off to work or to a meeting. She was becoming less and less able to visit for any length of time.

That June, I went to New York to meet with the senior managers at the Health Department, when I started feeling terribly sick. I thought I had eaten something that didn't agree with me. I went to the ladies' room to gather my composure. When I opened the door, there were several EMTs standing there. They started to examine me. I thought it was really strange for them to barge in like that, just because I had indigestion.

I guess I'd been in the washroom for a long time. I thought it was a few minutes. They insisted it was 20 minutes. "Let's not quibble over a few minutes," I tried to joke.

But they weren't buying my lighthearted routine. "We are taking you to the hospital," they informed me.

"But I have this meeting to go to," I said, with what was apparently a lopsided smile. They put me on a stretcher and started to carry me out of the building. The entire staff was standing along the hall. I was, of course, sitting up, waving like Queen Elizabeth and vowing to return shortly. I was thinking they had hailed a cab and we would ride to the hospital. I was shocked to see an ambulance waiting to carry me off to the hospital. Once again, I couldn't believe what was happening. How could these otherwise competent professionals be so crazy as to use an ambulance for a case of heartburn?

They kept insisting that they suspected I had had a stroke. I clearly disagreed with this diagnosis, though the doctors at the hospital told me they were going to keep me for a few days to monitor my condition. My condition? Why would you monitor indigestion for three days in a New York City hospital? No way. They completed the scans and blood tests and several serious-looking doctors examined me and told me I would be staying with them for a while and that the commissioner had called to be sure I was under expert care. None of this made any sense to me. So against their orders, I checked myself out of the hospital and caught the 4:20 train back to Albany.

JOHN: Denial runs in the family, obviously.

JOYCE: Jamie and John were at the station to meet me. Jamie was obviously very concerned and feeling very guilty, thinking that she was responsible for causing me so much stress.

JAMIE: I was feeling guilty and terrible and scared. I felt like I was in a real trap. I didn't see any way out of my addiction. I knew about recovery. I knew about the steps. But in AA, they say that people are constitutionally incapable, and that was the way I felt. I felt like I was dying and I couldn't stop.

When my mom got off the train, I was petrified. I was so relieved that she was alive, but I was really worried and scared and sad and guilty and not sure what was going to happen next.

I can't even begin to go back and re-create what I was thinking at that time, because I wasn't *thinking*. At that time, if I wasn't high, I was thinking about how to get my next high. The obsession to use had taken over everything. The ways and means to get more became all I could think about. There was nothing rational at this point in my using that I can look back on.

JOYCE: This was the first time that John and I shared denial. I was in deep denial about what had happened to me. I was refusing to agree with the chief of neurology and the commissioner of health, who were both insisting that I had had a stroke. I knew that something had happened, but I didn't want to know what it was.

JOHN: The doctor came over the next day, sat down at our table, looked Joyce straight in the eyes and said, "You've had a stroke."
Joyce said, "No, I didn't." She was in complete denial.

JOYCE: Frankly, I just knew I couldn't afford the time or the energy to be sick.

TEN

. . . .

When the Dealing's Done

JOYCE: Jamie was seeing a therapist who was still saying she was going to be all right and she wasn't in any danger of hurting herself.
Again, I was feeling scared and wasn't agreeing with her—but what
did I know?

I was picking Jamie up every morning to go to work. She was
working near me and didn't have a parking space, so I'd call her to
wake her up before I left home.

One morning she didn't answer the phone, so I drove over to her
condo and knocked. When there was no answer, I let myself in.

There was a bottle of vodka on the table. Jamie was sound asleep.
When I woke her up, she said the bottle wasn't hers, it belonged to her
friends who were sleeping in the next room. I burst into their room
and pulled them up, told them to get out. I screamed at them, saying
that alcohol would kill Jamie. I got into the car, called Jamie's therapist,
who said, "Calm down; everything is okay." But I was livid. It turned
out that this fellow was her dealer and his girlfriend was a friend.

JOHN: I thought Joyce was unbelievably courageous. The way Joyce dis-
plays her love is simply amazing. She will do whatever it takes to

right an injustice. She will stand up to a perceived danger and take it head-on, especially if the danger is right in front of her. She took an incredible risk. She threw them out. That was the amount of love she had for Jamie.

JAMIE: The guy was my drug dealer. He was 28 and his girlfriend was 18. He was living with me and paying rent. When he paid rent, I used the money to get high.

JOYCE: I didn't know until just this moment that he was living there, in our condominium.

JAMIE: Well, it was only for a month. At that point, when my mom came in, I probably had fallen asleep only an hour before. I remember thinking I was caught again, but the crack was so powerful that any logical emotion or thought was cut off. The drug dealer and his girlfriend felt bad and wanted to apologize to my mom. They didn't normally drink around me.

JOYCE: At that time, I had no idea that he was a dealer. I thought he was just another friend. He was actually very gentle. He looked at me with such a sad expression. Looking back, I think I could have been killed doing what I did, screaming at him the way I did. Picking up a gang member by his shirt and pushing him out of the room was maybe not a smart idea.

JAMIE: Things were obviously becoming more and more serious. I had another friend, K, who was my best friend in high school. I hadn't been in touch with her since I had been using. Her brother was a police officer. The drug dealers used to take my car and one night I got a call from her brother. One of the guys had taken my car and had been stopped by the police. My friend's brother said, "Jamie, I'm really worried. These are really, really bad guys and you don't want to hang around with them."

K completely stopped talking to me at that point. I went back to see her when I was in recovery to do my amends. She told me that her brother had *never* meddled in her business before then, but he had called and told her that I was hanging out with very dangerous people. She said she had decided that if I was choosing to be with those people over her, she just had to stop talking to me.

JOHN: We didn't know anything about this conversation K had with her brother. But I remember one night I saw Jamie's car where I knew the dealer lived. As I approached, the car took off. I chased that car as far as I could through the streets of Troy. I didn't think she was not in the car. I went home saddened to the depth of my soul. The grief that I felt was not one of feeling victimized as much as just so sad for her, Joyce and me that our lives had come to this. A great sorrow was swelling in my heart. However, I could still feel an inner strength that lifted me and somehow soothed me as much as I allowed it to.

JAMIE: There was another time that I owed the drug dealers money and I didn't know how I was going to pay them. They threatened to kill me, so I had to talk to my dad. I did tell him that it was for drugs, but I didn't tell him that it was for crack. He wound up meeting the dealer and paying him the money, because he was serious.

JOHN: What could I do? It was my kid. Let her get killed? You know, therapists say, all the time, that you have to put your foot down. Throw your kid out, stop talking to them, whatever. But how could we do that, especially when, if we did throw Jamie out, if we didn't pay the dealer, there was a strong possibility she would be killed? And we could have prevented her death. I could not live with that.

JOYCE: It was terrifying and heartbreaking that John had to go and pay this guy. Before he went, he wrote a note to give the dealer. In it, he said that he knew the drug dealer was a better person than that, and he knew there was hope. He said that he hoped one day the dealer would look back on this moment and realize that someone cared for him. One part of me thought, "My god, my husband and my daughter are just out of their minds." But the other part of me was amazed at John's ability to respond to this situation from a spiritual perspective. And I respected that.

JOHN: I was consistent, at least. I was trying to hold the high road. I believed that it was the right thing to do.

I remember writing that note. I remember thinking about what I wanted to say. I remember wanting to keep focusing on the light. I knew that it was a horrible thing to be a drug dealer. Money was good, but the life was terrible—I knew that. Dealers aren't going around building good relationships with people. They see their clients as objects. The dealer cannot allow himself or herself to know the effects of the drug use on their clients, their families and the children in their families. They have to disconnect from that in order to make the deal. They become part of the living dead of our society. I was determined not to condemn the drug dealer. I wanted to use the opportunity as a way for him to think about what he was doing.

I thought in some way this note might be the beginning of his questioning what he was doing, that it might prevent one dealer from dealing to another parent's child. I did not want, in any way, to have my thoughts contribute to the hate, greed and hunger of people's souls by condemning him. It was not because I was on such a high moral ground but because it was the practical thing to do. Studies have shown that our thoughts and prayers travel across time and space and can have an impact. I wanted to influence this person in some positive way that was consistent with my integrity.

The note was so out of character for a payment to a drug dealer. I just hoped he would read it.

JOYCE: Jamie told us many times during subsequent years that the dealers were always telling her they didn't want her to use. I think it was because with her there was some kind of personal connection, some small bit of a relationship.

These were the things that kept us strong, gave us hope, kept the purpose alive. We could see that there was a way out of the despair. We would ask ourselves, "What are we called to do in this situation?"

JOHN: We could always control who we were and how we were going to go through this. We couldn't control what Jamie was doing, but we could control the way we responded. We could control what we thought and what we kept in our hearts.

JAMIE: Later, my dealer said to me that no one had ever said anything like that to him. Never. Obviously, Dad's note had some impact on him.

Another Bad Draw

JOYCE: One late-summer day, a man showed up in our front yard while I was gardening. He was a bit scary looking. He said, "Hi. I met you years ago and I'm looking for Jamie."

JAMIE: When I met J a few years earlier, I was bartending at a rural bar. He used to bang his empty glass on the counter when he wanted another drink. One day I turned around and said that for every time he banged his glass, he'd have to wait another minute for his next drink. He said, "Do you talk to all your customers like that?"

I said, "No, only the assholes."

To which he replied, "I'm going to marry you."

He was always saying that he was going to marry me. He told my mom and dad. He told everyone. But he screwed up and went to jail for several DWIs and evading a police officer. He had a long history with the police, which I didn't know at the time. I hadn't seen him for years.

He was a very handsome guy. He had jet-black hair, sea-blue eyes and a fabulous body. I thought he was an incredibly good-looking man. When I first met him, I found him very attractive, but I knew that he was an alcoholic. Back then, I didn't know that I was, too. So we hung out a bit early on and he used to bail me out regularly. But there was no intimacy. He wrote to me while he was in jail. He said, "I'm going to find you when I get out and we'll connect up." He called me Sunflower. So the day he got out, he came to my house and picked me up. We went to a Chinese restaurant and we talked and I gave him my number.

JOHN: He seemed to be Jamie's type. He was strong, handsome, a good worker. I thought he would look after her. Notice I omitted the fact that he was a felon. However, I thought everybody deserved another chance. As I reread this, I wonder if I am ever going to get this—the lack of protection I gave Jamie by not saying "What's wrong with you? Look at what you are choosing. It's simply astonishing to me." However, I don't think she would have listened, anyway. But in retrospect, I should have said it. I felt like a guardian of sorts, standing by her, witnessing her decisions, loving her through them and interfering where I could make the most impact and hoping for the best. It is so hard to watch a person you love systematically destroy herself. Hard as it was, both Joyce and I were sustained by our spiritual practice. We made an effort to nourish ourselves and hold the light for her so she did not get so lost that she would not be able to find her way back. We did this for ourselves as much as for Jamie.

JAMIE: But I was sick, and J was sick. We wound up talking about drugs and that sort of stuff. Once we talked about what we were doing, it opened up a Pandora's box. When we found out that we were both using, we started using together.

JOYCE: I remember it like a photograph. When I turned around and this guy was standing there, my stomach flipped over and I thought, "Oh, no, just when I thought that things were as bad as they could get, they just got worse." I remembered meeting him years before at the bar where Jamie worked. He was so drunk that I couldn't understand a word he was saying. It was sad. I felt very sorry for him. And now he was back. I was sure that he had to be clean, because he was going back and forth to jail. Maybe there was hope. Maybe he would help her. Maybe if she saw the consequences of drinking, she'd see things differently.

JAMIE: He was a gifted mason and he had his own company; so when he got out of jail, he had no problem getting work. He was also a gifted handyman.

He was a con artist. He was extremely manipulative. Here's an example: Anyone who goes into a car dealership to buy a car has to show a valid driver's license. He goes in with no license, with jail time for DWI, and comes out with a car.

JOHN: He was over at the house that day, and asked me if I wanted to go with him to get the vehicle. I said, "How are you going to get this truck? You just got out of jail for DWIs, you have no license, you have a questionable history—how are you going to do this?"

He said, "Don't worry about it; I'm good." I saw him conning the salesman. He simply said, "Oh, I don't have my driver's license with me, but I'm good." I couldn't believe it. But I also didn't know exactly how bad his history was. I have no idea how he did it.

JOYCE: This guy had been convicted of aggravated unlicensed operation of a motor vehicle. He had nine DWIs and he was continuing to drive without a license. To add insult to injury, someone sold him a car—a brand-new Ford truck. How does that happen?

JAMIE: He could con a con artist, sell ice to an Eskimo.

JOYCE: And do it well. Within two weeks of his showing up at our house, he moved in with Jamie.

JAMIE: On August 5, 2001, I wrote in my journal that we had been together for five days and we'd had six fights. Once he moved in, he began writing in my journal. He always wrote things such as he would never leave me, he loved me, he just wanted to take care of me.

JOYCE: He was writing in your journal. No indication of a problem there!

JAMIE: On August 25, he brought his beautiful children from his former marriage to the condo for a visit. As soon as they came over, I went out. I guess I couldn't face the responsibility. I met up with some people I knew at a bar and started using. I just went there to get a little weed and have a juice while I waited. But, as we say in the program, "Hang out in the barbershop long enough and you're gonna get a haircut." And once I started, I couldn't stop.

JOYCE: Jamie was telling me at that point that she thought children were a big responsibility and that having them around would save her from drinking. Then they came over and she left and went drinking. While I didn't know at the time that it was happening, I am sorry to hear about it now. It still doesn't make any sense, unless you know that this disease moves in and hurts everyone it touches. And it's very good at not making distinctions between who it will take down and who it won't. The Beast will take everyone!

JAMIE: I was gone for a day. I went out the first afternoon and didn't go home until the next afternoon. At that point, I started going back to AA, but I was really depressed. I hated life, and J and I were fighting a lot.

ELEVEN

The Terrorist Attack

JOYCE: It was a few minutes after nine o'clock on the morning of September 11, 2001, when Jamie called. She was the one who told me that a plane had crashed into the World Trade Center. I was on the executive staff of the Department of Health, so I had to go to work. I think I talked to Jamie about 32 times that day. Because everyone was in shock, everything was surreal. Her behavior didn't seem strange to me, but she was in a manic state about this tragedy and was experiencing post-traumatic stress at the same time.

When I got home, we called her and begged her to come over. We spent an hour and a half on the phone with her, but she said she was too tired to get out of her warm bed and drive over. We said good night to her at 11 p.m.

The next morning, I went to work and carried on. Jamie hadn't answered the phone that morning, so I called John and said that I was worried and asked him to check on her at the condo.

JOHN: When I got there, she was vomiting. I said, "You went out and drank, didn't you?" She said yes. I was so disgusted with her. In the middle of this enormous tragedy, what did she do? She went out and drank. The whole nation was upside down and all she could think about was drinking. My clinical skills went out the window along with my compassion.

JOYCE: I got home from work around 6:30. We were just about to take a walk when the phone rang. It was a call from one of Jamie's childhood friends. She said, "Joyce, I've just called the police. Jamie took a whole bottle of Tylenol PM last night and she won't go to the hospital."

I called the condo immediately and J answered. He said the cops were there and they were going to take her to the hospital. I asked if they could wait for me. They said, "No, ma'am. We're taking her now."

JOHN: We rushed to the emergency room as Jamie was being taken to the hospital with a police escort. Her boyfriend was denying that anything was wrong. He didn't want her to go to the hospital at all.

JOYCE: When we got there, Jamie was angry with everyone. She was furious that someone had called the police. She was lying to the doctor about everything—her weight, her medical history. She was belligerent with us and everyone on the staff. I said, "This is not the first time she's tried to hurt herself."

She said, "That's not true; you're lying."

I said, "I'm not lying; you've done this before."

It was as though someone else were going through this, not I. It was as though I were looking at a person I didn't know. She wasn't my daughter. But she *was* my daughter.

She had to take a medication that would detoxify her liver. It made her very sick. She did let me into the bathroom while she was ill and we were up all night long at the hospital with her while they did everything to detoxify her 89-pound body.

There I was, with this stranger giving her this poison to try to save her life. She was admitted to the hospital in the morning and she remained there for five days with a police guard. They were on suicide watch. I think it took us two days to realize that this was what was happening. For the next several days, we took shifts being with her at the hospital. On September 14, Jamie's 29th birthday, they told her that they were going to discharge her from the hospital and admit her to the psychiatric ward.

We moved her, her birthday roses and gifts down to the psych ward, where they put her in a locked area. There were people screaming, pulling their hair out, throwing lit cigarettes at one another; and there she was.

JOHN: To place your child, however old, in a locked psychiatric ward is a horrible experience, no matter how good the staff and the hospital are. It's something you can't conceive of in your worst nightmare. However, Jamie was safe for the moment. Things were breaking down so fast now; and it was her birthday. She just looked at us and said, "Thanks a lot. Thanks a lot for putting me here." We left and looked back at her through the bars and went home and cried ourselves to sleep.

JOYCE: Every year on the morning of Jamie's birthday, I wake up and relive the labor and her birth and looking at her for the first time. This year, though, all I could think was, "How did we get here?"

JAMIE: The morning of 9/11, I was sitting on the couch. I had turned on the Today Show and I saw it all happen. I wrote it all down in my journal. Sometimes people who are traumatized are drawn to things that are traumatic. It's called a trauma bond. They relive their own trauma through another event. Maybe they're looking for an explanation or for something to identify with.

Amid all this chaos and destruction, J reacted by calling me "white trash." We were fighting with each other while the World Trade Center was imploding.

I watched all day as they replayed and replayed and replayed the event. For the most stable person, this was unnerving. For people like me, it was unbearable. It was catapulting me into a severe depression or, worse, a catatonic state.

A couple of people called and said, "Why don't you come over and we'll hang out." I had a drink with them. When I went home, I was totally out of it. I was catatonic. I couldn't bear to feel anymore, so I took a bottle of pills. But I called someone. She lived in South Carolina. She was an alcoholic.

I fell asleep. When I woke up, everything was blurry. I remember that my father came in. I remember looking at him and talking to him and thinking, "Why does he not know I'm a mess?"

JOHN: I knew Jamie was a mess, but I thought she had a hangover and I was so disgusted with her that I just had to leave.

JAMIE: All I could do was sleep that day. I was so sick and groggy. But I did call my childhood friend. Then there was a knock on the door. J answered it. It was the police. They said, "You need to come with us, ma'am."

I said, "I don't think so."

They said, "Yeah, you do." They said, "Did you take some pills?"

And I said, "Yes, I did."

They said, "Well, you can't do that." Who knew that you weren't "allowed" to do that? But it comes back to the fact that addicts don't think it's about anything but them. They said, "You can come with us in the police car or go in the ambulance." So I got myself together and went with them.

I was so angry. I was so angry that someone had told on me. I was just so angry that I was consumed. I thought that I was at the end of the road. I felt that I was being forced against my will to do something, and I didn't want that, even though I prayed to God every night to help me.

When I got to the hospital, they started to force me into detoxing. The next thing I remember is that when I woke up, the doctor came in and I told him, "I'm going out for a cigarette."

He said, "No, you're not."

I said, "Yes, I am; I'm going out for a goddamn smoke."

He said, "We don't use that kind of language here, ma'am—would you like me to call the authorities?" At that point, I didn't care who he called. I really don't remember much else about the rest of the hospital stay—until it was time to be released.

Then they moved me to the psych ward. It was a locked room with two beds. I lay down and looked across at the girl in the bed next to me. She was very big, very huge. Her back was toward me. I thought, "Oh, my god, she's going to kill me." I was scared; and I was still angry. I wanted to blame someone for doing this to me.

I felt like it was a conspiracy that my parents were involved in.

JOYCE: It was. It was a conspiracy to keep her alive.

JAMIE: And the girl who called in on me was part of it as well. At that time, my mind was gone. I was devoid of any rational thinking. It was a strange thing, because I was so in the moment, taking it minute by minute, that I almost had no thoughts. I belonged there, because I was insane. They gave me Adavan, which numbs and medicates you; so I slept.

JOYCE: The next morning, I got up and went to work.

JAMIE: Mom has always been a crusader for me. She always takes care of everything. In a weird, sick way, it was the reason part of me always felt that I was safe, even when I was at my worst.

JOYCE: Something changed for me that day. I had known for a while that I was at risk of losing my daughter, but now I wasn't even sure that this was my daughter anymore. So the only thing I could do was to address the issues that I could: health-insurance coverage, intense meetings with the psychiatrist in charge of Jamie's case.

The night before this particular meeting with her, I dreamed that I was called to the morgue. They took me downstairs, pulled out a drawer and asked me to identify the body. It was Jamie.

When I reviewed the dream with the therapist, I had to confront the fact that Jamie could die at any moment and there was nothing I could do about it. It put me squarely on the first step of AA—I finally realized that I was powerless over this addiction.

With that admission came a sense of understanding that we were involved in a disease that was killing all of us—some parts of all of us. One of the things that came clearly to me was that I was as insane as my daughter, because I thought I could make her better.

It shattered the illusions that (a) it was about me and (b) she and I were the same person. I had to admit that we were separate.

All this time, in my mind, I was keeping her alive, which, of course, was ridiculous. But I felt it was my responsibility; it certainly was my passion and, of course, my failure. Now that I could look at her gone, I could see clearly that she was separate from me and that I could do absolutely nothing about it.

So I realized I was addicted, as well. I was addicted to rescuing Jamie, to being her protector. I was obsessed with it. Sitting at this table in a psych ward, with Jamie and the therapist, talking about her situation, was surreal. Jamie finally spoke up. "You know, my parents have always loved me, they have always done everything they could, and the more they love me and the more they do for me, the worse I feel."

A rage came over me. I said to her, "That really f.... us, doesn't it? How unfair is that, how twisted? Because if we don't do anything, you're going to die, and now you're telling us that if we do help you, we are putting a gun to your head."

Most of my professional life had been about creating possibilities for change, and now here I was, at the end of the road, obviously unable to effect any change in my own family. I couldn't create any more possibilities, because the only way I knew how to do it was to create through love. In this case, love was killing my daughter—or so she said. I was full of pain and hopelessness.

JOHN: At that time, I felt a renewed sense of safety. Jamie was with people who were looking after her, containing her so she couldn't hurt herself. I was so relieved not to be on edge about a phone call. At the same time, I could see that the love that we were giving Jamie was causing her pain, because she didn't think she was worthy of it.

JOYCE: Jamie was doing her best lying to the care workers at the psych ward. We wanted her to go into a full residential rehab. She was trying to persuade them to discharge her. So, while I had had this realization about my helplessness, I was still trying to get Jamie to choose life. I had taken the first step in the program, but I was still "using," I was still trying to save Jamie.

JOHN: But the psychiatrist who was working with Jamie saw the situation clearly. She knew exactly what was going on. She understood Jamie.

JOYCE: There was one really big step forward for me during this. The realization that I couldn't do anything to save my daughter helped me see her as a sick person, a person who was not me. Looking back at it today, I don't know whether I would do anything differently. I was committed to doing whatever it took. But having this realization that we were separate somehow relieved some of the pressure so I could care differently, I could go about the battle differently.

JOHN: When Jamie was admitted into the inpatient program, we finally thought we could sleep—at least for 28 days.

JAMIE: As I stayed longer in the psychiatric ward, I began to like the people there. They were supportive. They were just like me. I finally found a group that I fit into. I was home. So I felt a bit safer and I started to calm down. I behaved well. They moved me very quickly from the locked ward to the unlocked ward. I was still having panic attacks, but they would give me the Adavan and I'd be okay.

I was walking around the hall one day when a nurse pulled me into a room and sat me down. She said, "Jamie, you are walking around here with a smile on your face. Do you know where you are? I don't want you to be a frequent flier here," she said. "Some people come in and out and in and out, because there's a part of them that likes it here. You don't have to be one of those people. You are a special girl with a wonderful heart. Please learn from your experiences. You don't need to be here." And it wasn't only the professionals who were saying that to me. My roommate, Jessica, said it, too.

That night I had a panic attack. I couldn't breathe. The same nurse came in and sat with me as I went through it. She helped me breathe, red for in and blue for out. I saw the colors that night for the first time. She healed me. I felt it. I think about her a lot and about how much she helped me.

When I woke up the next day, I felt different. I said, "My god, she's right. Look where I am."

JOYCE: She liked the psych ward so much that she cried when we picked her up to take her to rehab. She kept running back into the ward. We had to get her escorted out.

JOHN: We had to escort her in and we had to escort her out. It's true; she didn't want to leave. She felt like she belonged there.

JAMIE: I loved it; it was nutso land. It was safe for me. I didn't want to go to rehab. No one walks into recovery brimming with happiness, hope, joy and love.

JOYCE: You wanted to be in a psych ward but you didn't want to go to rehab?

JAMIE: Maybe it was that I knew I was going to get treatment in rehab and I wouldn't get drugs like I was getting in the psych ward. Because they had identified me as bipolar and I was having the panic attacks, they'd give me drugs to keep me stable.

JOYCE: That was when John and I really started to set up boundaries. We told Jamie that we wouldn't pay for her psychiatrist if she didn't go to rehab.

JOHN: Joyce and I made a very clear decision that we were going to support only life-affirming decisions.

JAMIE: So I went. As soon as Mom and Dad made that shift and started setting those boundaries, I knew I didn't have a choice. I wasn't going to be able to go home again unless I was clean.

JOYCE: I was completely relieved. She was going into the 28-day program and was going to get better. I was thrilled.

So away we go, thinking what a hell of a thing to be proud of—finally got our kid into rehab, while our friends' kids were going to Harvard. What's wrong with this picture?

JOHN: As true as that was, there was also an element of truth in how proud we were of Jamie and ourselves for taking this momentous step. People without addiction issues in their family can have very little idea of the monumental toll it takes on family members on a day-to-day basis. This was cause for great celebration and relief.

JAMIE: The nurse in the psych ward told me that it wasn't going to be easy in the treatment center. She told me that it wasn't a dorm I was going to and if I wanted to get better, I needed to be introspective and do some work. She gave me a quote that I still remember—"The best revenge is living well."

JOYCE: So we dropped her off at rehab and drove away.

JOHN: We were exhausted.

JAMIE: As I walked up the stairs at the treatment center, I saw a big banner that read "Expect a Miracle." I thought, "Jesus, what's this all about?"

They took everything away—cigarettes, money, perfume, deodorant, makeup—everything. I had a ton of clothes that I had brought from the psych ward. It was a pain.

They walked me down to dinner and they told me I could sit outside and have a smoke. Two counselors came up to me and introduced themselves and told me how happy they were that I was there. I almost gagged. Another person came up and said the same thing. They were all telling me it was going to get better. It was going to get better; just wait. I wanted to scream at all of them! I went through the screening processes. The nurse in charge of meds and groups was a riot—he was a vivacious, engaging guy, overtly gay. I went into the office and said to him, "I need to leave."

He said, "Why?"

I said, "I just need to leave." I had cats at home and I needed to take care of them.

He took me to the office to talk to the director. I was crying. I said again, "I don't need to be here."

A nurse said, "You don't need to be here? Let me ask you, have you ever broken a bone because of your drinking? Have you ever gotten annoyed when people bothered you about your drinking? Have you ever tried to stop? When was the last time you used? How much did you use? Were you able to stop once you started?" I answered all the questions and then he said, "And you don't think you have a problem?"

I said, "I have two cats at home who need me. I've got to go home."

JOYCE: There's absolutely no contact with inpatients for the first two weeks. We couldn't call Jamie or the counselors and they couldn't call us. It was a blackout period, so we didn't know what was going on with her.

JAMIE: The counselor said, "Maybe we can arrange for a home visit if you comply with all the rules. But not until after the two-week blackout. So," he said, "here's the deal; let's make a deal." And we addicts, we love deals. "So," he said, "let's just work on today. And tomorrow, we'll see."

So I went to my room and I went to bed.

Every day they said to me, "One day at a time." I started going to group sessions, but I was still angry, still insane. I went to this group and they showed a movie of people smoking crack. I was watching this and all of a sudden I was feeling the desire to use. I started raising my hand and being a pest. The group ended and I went up to talk to the counselors. At the same time, these two big girls started fistfighting, going at it hard. I thought I was crazy. I said I had to get out of there.

My boyfriend had left money at home in the condo. I knew where it was—under the computer. After the girls started fighting, I said, "I'm out of here." I called a cab from the pay phone on the floor. I packed my bags, snuck by the counselors and walked out. One of the counselors came running after me and said, "Where are you going?"

I said, "I'm out of here." And I left.

I used the money J had left for me at the condo to pay for the cab and get high. I called my dealer as soon as I paid for the cab. He came right over with the stuff I wanted. I sat in the condo and got high.

JOYCE: We had no idea about any of this, obviously, until she called us from the condo. Wait—she was calling us from the condo. What was she doing home? She told us that it was too dangerous in rehab, she had to get out for her own safety. "Oh, sure," I said, "it's much more dangerous than trying to kill yourself."

So the despair set in again, and the anger. I had to force myself to remember what I had just learned: I can't do anything about this. I can't do anything about this. All I can do is meditate and be still and trust God—between the incredible bouts of rage, when I just wanted to go over there and choke her, go over and hold her until she was free of The Beast who had taken her over. Where was my daughter?

John kept saying, "Just calm down; it's going to be all right." Then I wanted to choke him, too.

JOHN: I was furious, too, absolutely furious, but I had to focus on Joyce. I spent a lot of my effort trying to help Joyce calm down and enter her stillness. I just wanted her to be still, because that was where the comfort lay. And I knew she would then be okay. She was blowing a gasket a minute. Remember, she had just had a stroke and I did not want her to die. I was struggling, though, because the more I tried to comfort Joyce, the angrier she got. She was saying the same thing that Jamie had said to us—"The more you try, the angrier I get. Leave me alone."

JOYCE: I didn't have a stroke! But I gave up at that point. I couldn't do anything. "Jamie," I said, "you made the choice, you live with it." And I backed away and didn't talk to her for a while.

JOHN: Neither of us did. As tough as it was, 24 hours a day, waiting for the phone to ring in the middle of the night, wondering what she was doing, whether she was alive, we didn't call.

JAMIE: On October 16, 2001, my boyfriend got parole. He was out for good—until he went in again, of course. At that time, I was going to AA meetings; but I was still using, of course. I was on the fence, one foot in recovery, one foot out.

My boyfriend was living with me, but he was a mess. On October 30, I took a leave of absence from the job, because I was becoming even more of a mess with him around.

By the end of November, we were again using regularly together. One day, we kept paging our dealer and he didn't return the page. We called over and over again. We wanted drugs and we were getting desperate. We even drove by his house to see if he was home.

This was the dealer who had looked at me one day and said, "I hate to give this to you. You are such a good girl and you don't know what you are doing to yourself. I almost don't want to sell you this stuff anymore." He was the same guy who had been in the bedroom, who Mom had picked up by the collar and thrown out not too long before. He really was a nice guy. The next morning, we read in the paper that there was a murder in Troy. It was he, my dealer, and his girlfriend. They were violently murdered in their apartment. She was 18 years old; she was beautiful. They were massacred.

We were in shock. We had almost gone into the condo the day before, when we were so desperate to get our stuff. We could have literally walked in on them being killed. We couldn't believe it. We were in total shock. It was just crazy. Then we got scared. We thought, "My god, our number is in his pager. What if the police called us and started questioning us?"

JOHN: The whole community was in total shock about the brutality of their murder. We had no idea Jamie was connected to this guy. She gave us no indication whatsoever that she knew them. At this time, we had backed away from her a bit, so we may not have been in much contact with her. We certainly weren't conscious that she was deep in this horrible, brutal world. It was like it was just another story being played out on stage four instead of on stage one.

JOYCE: Did you feel anything for this man, your dealer, when all of this happened? I know even though I didn't realize who they were, my heart ached for them, for their families. The girl's parents were consumed with pain and I was identifying with them. Some part of me knew that girl could have been Jamie.

JAMIE: Oh, yeah, I felt real sadness. He didn't deserve that. Neither did his girlfriend. It affected me more than it affected my boyfriend. As they say in recovery, if the drugs don't kill you, the lifestyle will, and their murder made that statement a reality. I was still using, so my brain was fried. I realized, though, that now this was serious stuff, much more serious than all the other serious stuff I'd been through.

JOYCE: This is how absurd the whole thing was. What's more serious than a rape? A murder? Denial keeps all these things separate, as though they are unconnected events. Jamie couldn't see that one led to the other and it was a downward path—a path that would lead to a horrible death.

JAMIE: For the next couple of days after the murder, I continued to use. We started to get our drugs off the street, because the two other dealers I knew had gone to jail on drug charges.

I was struggling—I was still on the fence and my boyfriend was really unsupportive. He was not into AA—none of that. One day we got into a big fight. He said unbelievably horrible things to me. He said I deserved to be raped. He said that I would never amount to anything, because I always relied on my parents. He kept repeating all the same awful things he'd said to me many times before.

That day I went to a meeting. When I came home, he was drunk and asleep on the couch. The place was trashed. He had broken a coffee table. He had torn a pack of smokes apart. He had ripped up a book of mine and written all kinds of nasty things all over it.

I woke him up and when he opened his eyes, his hands went directly to my throat. I was trying to get away from him. He chased me around the condo, choking me. He stuffed a sock into my mouth so I couldn't scream. I thought he was going to kill me. I was pounding on the floor, trying to call for help. I finally grabbed a cactus plant and hit him over the head. That stunned him long enough for me to get out. He came chasing after me. I lost him somewhere along the way, and then I went back to the condo. I locked the door, thinking I was safe there, when I heard a crash. He had climbed up the outside of the building to our balcony, which was on the second floor, and he smashed the sliding glass door with his foot.

I ran downstairs and out of the condo. In a panic, I pounded on a neighbor's door. I said, "Please let me in; my boyfriend is going to kill me." I called the police and two guys from AA. As the police were taking my boyfriend away, he was yelling and accusing me of cheating on him with the friends who had come to help me.

The next morning, they let my boyfriend out of jail, and he came over. He said, "I want to go to a meeting with you." So we went. At the meeting, he raised his hand and said, "I almost killed my girl-friend last night."

I thought, "Well, maybe he really does want to go for help."

Then we started using again. I kept getting sicker each day, and I began to realize he wasn't ever going to get straight. I thought, "I'm probably going to die if I keep using like this." It is often said that you need to hit bottom before you can rise to a point of freedom. I knew I had had enough. Prior to this, I didn't care if I died. For the first time in a long, long time, I did care. I didn't think I had much to live for, but I believed a little bit that others could see something good in me. They believed that I could make it; they believed that I was someone who had something to offer; they believed in a higher power; they believed in hope—something I hadn't felt in a long time. I drew on their strength and *surrendered*. That was it; it was surrender. I was no longer riding the fence. I wanted it. I wanted hope, I wanted freedom, I wanted to break out of the prison in my own mind and let go of The Beast. I did the only thing I could think of: I called my parents and told them I needed help. I was ready to go back into the 28-day program.

JOYCE: Of course, we were thrilled to hear that; but we had been disappointed so many times before that we remained cautious in our optimism. We waited while she packed a few things and we drove her back to rehab.

JAMIE: So I was back in rehab. On the first day I heard this guy say, "I can't believe this place. It is outrageous."

I thought, "I'm going to be friends with him." He was a professional dancer who was very funny in a sarcastic gay way. Almost immediately we became very close friends.

Of course, my boyfriend came to visit me. One day, shortly after the two-week no-contact period was over, he took me outside and asked, "So, do you want to get married, or what?"

I just looked at him and said, "What?"

JOYCE: That, of course, was against all the rules. No relationships are allowed while you are in rehab.

JAMIE: I took the ring, anyhow. At group, I showed them the ring. They were in shock. They said, "You can't marry this guy; he hurts you. Give that ring back." At that point, I had started to talk, to tell the truth, so they knew something about this guy and they weren't going to let me do this. They told me to give the ring back, so I did. And he gave it right back to me. And I gave it back to him. It was like a bad comedy skit. It's the drama that takes place when the drugs are gone and you need something to replace them with.

I started to have a breakthrough around then. Although I was having to work really hard at my recovery, I realized it was good. I was stabilizing. Mom and Dad would come to visit me and I started telling them everything: I stole from them; I lied; it was crack I was using. I started telling them the truth.

JOYCE: We couldn't believe it. It was as though we were in one of those cartoons that portray a person with her head spinning and stars circling the brain. My god, when she started actually telling the truth, we realized that it was much worse than we ever thought.

JOHN: And what we thought was already bad.

JOYCE: We were so confused, but at the same time hopeful that she was going to get through it.

Because we didn't know everything that had happened, we thought it was okay for her boyfriend to come over to our house and visit while Jamie was in rehab. He was a con artist. He was always on the verge of tears, thanking us for caring about him. He kept telling us not to worry, that he was going to make it all okay, that he loved her and was going to take care of her. Then he told us he had given her a ring.

JOHN: We said, "Look, she's not ready, you're not ready, it's against the program rules. It's not the right time. Just take the ring back."

JOYCE: But, you know, we were talking about two adults; it was their lives. We kept trying to keep separate from them. There was a constant struggle in my head not to be in the middle of Jamie's problems anymore while, at the same time, having to pay for everything, literally. We thought getting engaged while in rehab was wrong—in fact, dangerous—but we knew that ultimately she would have to make her own decision.

Between that Christmas and New Year's, there was a warped sense of happiness. When Jamie was an inpatient, someone else could worry about her.

JOHN: I remember that Christmas. It was wonderful, in a weird kind of way—but there was finally what we thought was real hope. It felt safe to me.

JAMIE: I had a really good breakthrough in rehab. I got the principles of recovery instilled in my head. I finally understood that I had a toolbox that I could use. I started going to NA as well as AA. I knew I had to do 90 meetings in 90 days. And I started to like being clean. It was that there was hope. I had hope that life could be different. Being around people who had been through treatment and were back again was scary to me. I watched them carefully.

At one NA meeting with about 40 people, the counselor said, "Look around you. One or two of you are going to make it. Some of you are going to die." Some of the people were in really bad shape, living on the street, living with hepatitis, and it really opened my eyes. I was finally ready for it. I paid attention. I looked closely at what was going on around me. I decided that I didn't want to be like those people—back in rehab at 50 and 60 years of age.

They said, "Look, you don't have to do this, you don't have to be like us." They knew what it was like coming down off a crack high. I hadn't had that recognition in AA. This was a different environment. So I began to listen. I began to feel good.

One of my counselors kept telling me that I wasn't ready to get engaged. In one group session, he said, "What happened to you? Why are you here?"

I said, "Well, I'm here because I need help."

"No," he said, "why are you really here? What was it that drove you to use?" He was trying to get to the rape. He knew that there were things I didn't know that he knew. He was trying to get me to understand that I could feel and not have to use because of it. In recovery, they say that the best thing about it is that you feel again; and one of the worst things about it is that you feel again. But they teach you that you don't have to stay stuck in the feeling. Feelings aren't facts, but it's a fact that you're gonna feel. It will pass.

The really important thing about this part was that I was hanging out with people who understood me. And they loved me through it. I really began to feel that I was okay. I was being introduced to this new world of recovery that I didn't know existed. There were a lot of older people in AA. In NA, the people were younger. I felt at home. They were more like me.

JOYCE: She also was beginning to admit at that point that she was an addict. Even though she had gone through the motions before, she was still using. She was lying to herself and everyone else.

JAMIE: And the more I lied, the more I believed it.

JOYCE: She was so aligned with her denial that we couldn't see through it. She and her lying, up to that point, were very powerful together. That was the first time we heard her admit that she was an addict.

JAMIE: Until that time, I just thought I had a problem. I didn't know the problem had me. I ran into someone recently whom I knew from a school where I had taught when I was using. I said, "I'm doing really well now; I'm in recovery."

She said, "I'm glad you let the cat out of the bag."

I said, "Was it that bad?"

She said, "Well, let's just say that it was obvious there were problems."

JOYCE: When Jamie was graduating from the inpatient program, we wanted her to go into a residential program. I wanted her to stay away from that man. I tried really hard to get her to go, but she didn't want to. So when she was released in the middle of January, she went back home to the condo.

TWELVE

· · · · · · · ·

The Fallout

JAMIE: On Valentine's Day, 2002, a few weeks after I got home, J and I got into a rip-roaring fight. He left and came back with a Valentine present for me. It was a bag of crack.

I didn't want to use, but I had only 50 days clean. My mind was still addicted. I could resist it if I wasn't around it, but with a bag sitting right in front of me, I couldn't. And, of course, he knew this. He wanted me high. He knew he could have control over me if I was high. He knew that if I started getting clean, I'd leave. He knew that if I started getting better, I'd see how sick he was. He didn't like it when I went to meetings or when I talked to my friends in rehab. He hated it.

I relapsed that night. I knew it. I said, "I have to call everyone and tell them I relapsed."

He said, "No, you don't; you don't have to tell those people anything."

I said, "Yes, I do," and I did. I started calling people and telling them the truth. They came and got me and took me to a bunch of meetings. At one NA meeting, my counselor from rehab was there.

He started badgering me: "What are you doing with that guy? I can't believe you are with him."

His wife came up and said, "Hold on; you are crossing boundaries," and he stopped. What I realized, though, was that I still had this community, even though I had relapsed, and they still really cared about me.

THIRTEEN

Home Is Where the Heart Is

JOYCE: It was April sixth when Jamie called me and said she thought she was ready to go into the residential program, which was a six-to-nine-month program at a halfway house for women in recovery. Once again, I was hopeful and relieved and proud that she was really going to make a commitment to herself to get healthy both physically and emotionally. Then the phone calls started to come, the same phone calls we'd heard before: "I hate it here; these people are crazy. I hate it here; I want to get out."

JOHN: Despite her complaining, I was thrilled that she was in the program.

JAMIE: Two important things happened to me in the program. The first was that I met my current sponsor at a women's meeting where former addicts would come to support those in the program. I liked this woman's recovery story, so I went up to her and said, "Will you be my temporary sponsor?"

She replied, "Do you want temporary sobriety?" And she's been my sponsor ever since.

I kept telling her I wanted to leave the program and she kept telling me I had to stay, that this was where I was supposed to be. "Look down at your feet. This is where you are supposed to be." I was getting signs from everywhere that, as much as I hated it there, it was not a good idea to think about leaving.

The second thing was that I really struggled, because every day, I really wanted to get high and had to work through it. The residential program was located in a crack neighborhood. There were times the counselors had to hold me down, literally, so that I wouldn't walk out the front door and use.

I told this to one of the counselors one day. She sat me down and said, "Let's think this through to the end of what would happen if you did walk out the door right now." She took me through it step by step so I could clearly see the potential consequences. That was something I'd never been able to do before. She said, "Next time you see a deal going down, instead of looking at the deal, look at the pain in the person's eyes. Look at their eyes and see if you still want to use."

One day, some of the girls and I were out for a walk. We walked by a prostitute who was doing a deal. One of my friends said, "My god, that girl used to be my counselor. Holy god." I looked at her. She was really high. I looked at her eyes, as my counselor had told me to, and all I saw was excruciating pain.

A bit later, I was at a meeting, still talking about the same old stuff. I met up with a former counselor. When he heard me still talking about J, he said, "Jamie, you can't dance with the Devil and expect a miracle at the same time."

Every night when I was in the program, I wanted to get high. I cried every night. One particular night, I went into the cafeteria and said to the counselor, "I want to get high. I really, really want to get high."

She said, "You know what? I like you; you're going to make it. You aren't afraid to tell the truth. And as long as you tell the truth to the right people, they won't let you get high and you will make it."

JOYCE: Two months later, I was at my office in the Health Department. It was about one p.m., and I got a call. It was from the director of the program. She said, "She's gone. A white truck pulled up about an hour ago and Jamie left. She left with Mr. DWI." She said, "I'm so sorry; she was doing so well. She's going to be all right, but she's gone." I was furious. I could have taken that truck and run the both of them over.

JOHN: We were heartbroken—again. I didn't want to talk to Jamie, either. I couldn't. After I got over the heartbreak, I was furious. I was holding her boyfriend responsible. The road to recovery had taken another turn.

JOYCE: I called the condo and left a message. I told her that I could not speak to her. I didn't know when I would be able to speak to her. I couldn't watch her make the wrong choices anymore.

JAMIE: I was being a selfish bitch, thinking only of myself and, of course, of my boyfriend. I convinced myself the program was stupid, they didn't know what they were doing. I was still blaming others. I called my boyfriend and, of course, he came to get me. After we got back to the condo, he went to work and I called my mom. She wouldn't talk to me, which upset me. But I was determined that I was going to do the right thing.

Then I called my sponsor and told her. She wasn't happy with me, either. She told me to keep going to meetings, 90 meetings in 90 days, three meetings a day if I wanted. "You do the right thing and the right thing will happen," she kept telling me.

At one meeting, I met a guy named M. He'd say, "My name is M, but my friends call me truly blessed." It was my first experience with the affirmation of recovery, of people who truly got the essence of what someone could get from recovery. It was moments like that, moments that made me think differently, that kept me going to meetings continually.

One day, I picked up a girl I knew from the residential program. She needed a ride somewhere, but first we stopped at a corner store. As I sat there, a car went by and the horn started blowing. It was one of my drug dealers. He turned the car around and started driving toward me. All of a sudden, there was a person standing beside my window. It was M. I said, "You have no idea how happy I am to see you. You just saved me." I talked to M until he calmed me down and the dealer left. If the dealer had made contact with me, who knows whether or not I would have bought something? I continued going to meetings regularly.

While I was in the program, the dancer from rehab had moved into my condo with my boyfriend. So now the three of us lived together. He was clean, but I don't know about the boyfriend, whether or not he was clean during that time. But he knew by then that I was serious about my recovery. He was still very unsupportive of my being clean, but he knew I was determined to *stay* clean.

JOYCE: Jamie started having trouble with her boyfriend again. For the first time, we got an inkling that he might be physically pushing her around. Remember, we didn't know about all the other times. But she was covering for him.

JAMIE: He was always verbally abusive. I was relying on him financially, so he had me verbally, emotionally, financially—in every way. Right before this, my parents were on Cape Cod for a holiday. When they were away, we got a call from J's parole officer, who said that they knew he was abusing me. So they came and talked to us, checked out my body, my bruises, and asked a bunch of questions.

JOYCE: She was always calling us. This time she accused us of "tattling" on him. I was very angry with her. I was starting to worry that she was going to relapse, not make it in sobriety.

JOHN: And we did call the authorities. Of course we did.

JAMIE: Loverboy decided to look for a house for us to move into. Of course, he found one so far away that I couldn't be close to my friends. It was also too far to get to the AA or NA meetings that I had been going to. There wasn't much I could do about it, since he was controlling the money, so I went anyway.

JOYCE: Now, there is a good example of what the program calls "stinkin' thinkin'."

JAMIE: When we moved into the new place, I had a very uneasy feeling. I knew it wasn't good. I was still determined to stay clean. I was writing in my journal differently, but I was very cautious about what I was writing, because I knew he would read it.

One day he came home drunk. We started yelling and screaming and fighting. That's when I really, really knew I had made the wrong move. But my parents were still really, really mad. And I had too much pride: I couldn't go home.

On August 12, after J went out, I started to have a panic attack. He came back drunk again. He was violent. I called a friend, because I thought he was going to hurt me. I was talking to her and he was yelling in the background. We hung up and all of a sudden the police showed up. My friend didn't know my address but had called the State Troopers, who had called the police, who tracked me down. They made him leave. Then I left. I had ten cents to my name. I picked up my cats and my most important things and I called my parents. They were going to meet me at a gas station down the road, because I had no money and no gas.

While I was waiting for my parents, some of my boyfriend's friends showed up. I started to panic again, crying. I sat there in my car, sobbing, when a woman knocked on my window. She said, "Are you okay?"

I said, "No."

She said, "Why don't I get you an ice-cream cone?" She came back and sat with me until my parents showed up. When they did, she got out of the car and was gone. I didn't see her drive away; she just was gone.

JOYCE: So we went and picked her up, again. We just wanted to get her. It was the same mixture of conflicted feelings—furious/scared, hopeful/hopeless. We took Jamie home. She didn't know what she was going to do, just that she needed to be with us.

JOHN: I was working on a hypnosis CD at the time. We were sitting around the table, talking about what was going to happen next, and I said, "Why don't we listen to my CD together? I could use your feedback."

JOYCE: The next thing I knew, the CD was over, Jamie stood up and said, "I've got to go," and she left.

JOHN: We didn't know where she was going or what she was going to do.

JOYCE: About two hours later, she called from the house she shared with that man and said, "I'm moving out. Can you come and help me?"

JAMIE: Something in that CD propelled me to move, take a stand and get out.

JOHN: He was at the house when we got there, lying on the couch like a rag doll, playing the victim, as usual.

JOYCE: I remember threatening him, telling him to stay away from her or we'd get him thrown back into jail.

JAMIE: My friends and I had arranged for a U-Haul, which was there when Mom and Dad showed up. We got everything out in one day. You would think that would be the end of that relationship. At that point, he had almost killed me, we had fought all the time, I had moved out of his house. But I couldn't keep away. I continued to see him.

JOYCE: I think that if I had known that then, I may have tried to kill them both.

JAMIE: The writing in my journal was beginning to take on a more positive tone. Instead of starting out with everything that was going wrong, what I had to do to change my life, how I was making bad choices, I started out my journaling with what I was grateful for. Part of me had made a significant shift. It was now about getting the behavior to follow and about getting out of this destructive relationship. I knew this intellectually.

As I was visiting him, I kept going back and forth in my mind. I knew I needed to completely break away from him, but I was finding it very difficult. I also remember saying to myself that I wanted to have his baby. I even said it out loud to him and wrote it in my journal. So, at this early point in my recovery, I wasn't using drugs, but I was still addicted to old compulsive behaviors. I certainly wasn't thinking clearly. I was back living in my parents' condo. I got a job babysitting for a couple in Clifton Park. They were great people, with two kids.

On September 14, 2002, my 30th birthday, J took me to an inn in Vermont. After dinner, we went back to the room. I had been talking about healthy issues, about going to meetings, about priorities and goals. He never liked it when I talked about those things. He was like Jekyll and Hyde: He would say that he wanted to be supportive, but when I started to eat good stuff, he would get mad and tell me I couldn't do it, that I was no good.

He got so mad that night that he smashed my cell phone, stamped on it and broke it into pieces. As I watched him, I thought, "What is wrong with me? What am I doing with this person?" I had found some hope for the future, but I still didn't believe in myself enough to do it alone. I'd never been alone. It's the typical addict mind-set: I want love, but I'll accept anything. Something is better than nothing. I want real love, but I don't want to be alone and wait for it to show up.

JOYCE: We had totally cut J off. We had told him he wasn't welcome in our home and that we didn't want to see him at all. We had no idea Jamie was still seeing him at that point. I didn't ask her, I just assumed she wasn't. We were happy she was working with children again. We thought she was clean and she was, for the first time. We were starting to see a difference in her.

JAMIE: During that time, I was really dedicated to my recovery, so I was, for the most part, behaving differently.

On September 20, J and I had another fight at his place. I left and went home to my condo. He kept calling me, harassing me. In my journal, I wrote that I was scared of him, that he was stunting my growth.

Then, on October seventh, I found out that I was pregnant. I was getting up in the morning and throwing up. Despite this, I was always on time for my babysitting job, which started at 8:30 a.m. The woman I was babysitting for had an extra pregnancy test at home. So I took it. When I saw the little line that showed positive, a ton of feelings ran through me. All my life I had wanted to be a mother. I loved children, so I was happy about that. But I knew, in my heart of hearts, that it was not supposed to be with this man, who did not want me to stay sober. I was new in recovery, working only half days, and had very little money. I was so conflicted.

JOYCE: While this was going on, we were away visiting a friend for a three-day weekend. We were getting phone calls from Jamie and I was getting frustrated with her. We were beginning to think she was seeing this guy, again, and we didn't trust her. We didn't trust her sobriety. As always, we were completely obsessed with Jamie. For those three days, all we did was talk about her and about what we should be doing. She called and told us that she had something exciting to tell us when we got home. We thought, "Oh, great; she's going to marry him."

When we got home, she was looking through her baby books, saying, "Look how cute I was."

I said, "What's going on?" That's when she told us she was pregnant. My first response was, "What are you thinking? I know that you've always wanted a child, but you're still a child yourself. How are you going to take care of this baby?" At the same time, I was biting my tongue, because she was still very fragile. And this was going to be my grandchild; I knew I had to be careful about what I said. I felt like my head was going to blow off. I knew what this was going to mean to my life, to the commitment I'd have to make to ensure that this pregnancy went through safely.

JOHN: I felt very conflicted. It was certainly not the way I had hoped to hear I was going to be a grandfather. However, I knew how Jamie felt about it and I wanted to be happy for her, even though there would most likely be many perils along the way.

JAMIE: My mom said to me, "You're going to have a baby? How are you going to do this? How are you going to take care of yourself and this baby?"

All I could think was, "Couldn't she just support me, be happy for me?" This was what I'd wanted all my life. She made logical points, but I had a program, I had a sponsor, I thought I'd be okay. I was fortunate for this, because it gave me the support that I needed.

JOHN: She was still on meds for the post-traumatic stress and the recently diagnosed ADD. I remember that Joyce asked her if she was well enough to have the baby. She said yes, she was strong enough to have the baby.

JOYCE: It was an absurd situation. She was still so sick herself. She wasn't self-sufficient. She was financially and probably emotionally incapable of managing this. Yet she wanted to be pregnant, even while her body was still ravaged from the drugs and the drinking.

But at that point, I realized it was not my choice, I could not speak about it anymore. I was going to be a grandmother. Now it was my responsibility to be the best grandmother I could be. It was the last time I ever spoke about how outlandish the situation was; and I walked right into this illusion of hers. I committed to support her through it, to continue to help get her well so she could give birth to a healthy baby. I picked up the phone and made an appointment for her with my OB-GYN.

JAMIE: On October 12, Mr. Wonderful and I got into another fight. I had gone over to his place. I couldn't tell whether or not he had been drinking, because he could hide it really well. We started fighting. He told me that the baby probably wasn't even his. I stood up and he pushed me. I looked at him and said, "You know what? You just touched me and this baby for the last time. Do not try to contact me, do not try to contact this baby, do not call me, stay away. You've seen me and this baby for the last time." And I got into the car and drove away.

When I left him that night, I knew. I had found a piece of hope and run with it. There was something bigger than me now—the baby. The baby was my higher power that night. Maybe I didn't care enough about myself to protect me, but I cared enough about this baby to protect it. And I had no hesitation in protecting it from harm.

The program says, "You keep coming around, and we're going to love you until you start loving yourself." And at that point, I started to love myself. It was a combination of things: I was in recovery, I was clean, I had a therapist, I was on new meds, my mind was getting clear, I was going to meetings, I had a great sponsor. I now wanted to live significantly more than I wanted to die.

JOYCE: She was aware of it, aware of wanting to live. And she now had this baby to give her a reason, a purpose.

JOHN: The love that she felt for the child was going to be a much stronger motivation for her recovery than all of the logical, rational reasons we had been presenting to her.

JOYCE: Any rational person would have said that it was a ridiculous thing to do—to continue with the pregnancy. On the other hand, every situation has a redeeming opportunity, something that will make the experience all worthwhile. We had to think about it that way, that this was the catalyst for getting our daughter back.

JAMIE: Now my gratitude list was starting with things such as, "I'm grateful for not being nauseated and I'm grateful to have woken up one more day alive." It was a big shift for me.

J started harassing me, following me around, driving by the condo, calling me at all hours. I went to the police to file a complaint. They said, "Well, you've called before. Are you sure you want to go through with this?" I said yes. Luckily, I had saved the messages he was leaving, so I could start documenting his calls. There has to be a certain level of threat, a certain number of complaints, before the police will take the situation seriously and issue an order of protection.

JOYCE: You'd think that since he was on parole, they'd call his parole officer. We didn't know that Jamie had been seeing him through the previous few months. We wanted the police to call the parole officer immediately, but we didn't know how many times she'd called the police before about him. It wasn't making sense to me. But I also realized that she needed to handle this herself, so John and I backed off.

JOHN: It was important for us to back off, to keep out of this part of the drama. We would support her life decisions but not make them for her.

JAMIE: I got a restraining order and the next day I called the parole officer. Both she and the police told me it was very hard to prove someone was stalking me. Basically, I couldn't do anything without pictures or other proof. The parole officer told me that I'd have to go in and testify against him at the parole hearing. I started going to meetings for women in domestic-violence situations. In the meantime, he was still harassing me. The parole hearing wasn't going to be for another five months or so and I was getting more and more scared.

One morning, I went to McDonald's. I looked in my rearview mirror and there was his truck, following me. I pulled up to the drive-through, thinking I could scream something and someone would help me. He was throwing Hallmark cards at me. I was yelling into the speaker, "Leave me alone!" He threw the cards and then took off. He was a lunatic.

JOHN: We were so proud of Jamie for sticking to her principles, and yet were frightened for her because of the continued violations. The local police were extremely helpful to us, but the laws governing this type of situation were very clear. It's difficult to protect someone from a stalker.

JOYCE: The baby, whom Jamie had named Hannah, was due in June. Jamie was still babysitting for the family. It was the first Thanksgiving since she was in high school that Jamie came to the house on time for a holiday dinner. The same was true for Christmas. She was looking so healthy. We were beginning to feel like we had more control, that we were going to have a new chance at having a life as a family. The last time this guy called was on New Year's Eve.

JAMIE: I recorded his message on my cell phone. But that night, we were in a different county, so I couldn't call the police. He had been violating the restraining order all along and I was finally getting enough proof to show that he had been. I had gone online with the phone company and got a printout of the calls that were coming from his cell number, so I now had proof. I took the printout to the police station and that's when I had to go to court to get an order of protection, which was a three-year, completely stay-away order. It was in the spring of 2003.

JOYCE: He was there in the back of the courtroom with his head down, again acting like a victim. Going to court was part of our strategy to get him out of her life completely. We were showing him that we were willing to go as far as possible with the legal system to keep him out of Jamie's life. Originally, we had wanted him to go to jail because he was violating the restraining order. When we went to court, the lawyers negotiated his staying out of jail if he stayed away and complied with the order of protection. And he didn't want to go back to jail.

JAMIE: Yet he proceeded to violate the order. I once again called the police and had to go to court. My roommate at the time went with me. It ended up that J had to go back to jail for violating the first order of protection. When he got out, of course, the restrictions were even tighter. He kept going in and out of jail, but I wasn't in contact with him anymore.

JOYCE: One day, as Jamie was getting ready for Hannah's birth, she was cleaning up the condo.

JAMIE: There was a storage shed outside. I was talking on the phone with my mom as I was cleaning.

JOYCE: All of a sudden, she said, "What's this?" Then I heard, "Oh, my god!" She had found a sawed-off shotgun. I told her not to move, not to touch the handle of the gun, to stay still and I would send John over right away.

JAMIE: When my dad got there, he took the gun and drove off with it on the front seat of the car.

JOHN: I couldn't believe it. I thought, "Oh, Jesus, what else could happen?" There was a frickin' sawed-off shotgun in a golf bag in my daughter's shed, and I knew that there was only one reason it was there. It was just another unbelievable example of what occurs in the lifestyle of drug users. The violence that surrounds the drug trade is merciless. It takes no prisoners.

JOYCE: I was waiting on pins and needles for John to return home when I got a call from the police. "We've got your husband. He's here with this fully loaded sawed-off shotgun. He says it's not his. Can you attest to that for him?"

"Oh, my god," I said, "it's loaded?"

"Yes," they said, "and he's lucky he didn't blow his head off driving it over."

JAMIE: The serial number on the gun was scratched out. We found out later that the gun was wanted in a shooting. And I had no idea how that thing had got there.

FOURTEEN

. . . .

Life Anew

JAMIE: I was doing well with my sobriety. The pregnancy was going well. Everyone in recovery was very supportive. I quit smoking cigarettes and went to the gym. I was very healthy. I felt fabulous when I was pregnant and it had been a long time since I'd felt that way.

JOYCE: As spring approached, we began preparing the condo for the baby's arrival. We painted every room, installed new carpeting and converted the second bedroom to a beautiful nursery. The condo had become a different place. We wanted to wash away the horrible memories of the past and create a new home for Jamie and her baby. I moved into full-time grandmother mode. I had turned 55 and decided it was time to devote myself to helping Jamie stay sober and assuring the healthy birth of my granddaughter. I retired on April 1, 2003, so I could be present for Jamie during the last few months of the pregnancy. We spent time together every day, walking, talking, getting to know each other and preparing for a new life. We were full of hope. Soon we would welcome a new baby, experience profound joy and begin a whole new phase of our life as a family.

JAMIE: Throughout the pregnancy, I had been in an outpatient program. It was very helpful. I was at the condo one afternoon when the doorbell rang. I was about eight months pregnant. I opened my door and there was my former drug dealer. I couldn't believe it. I let him in and sat him down. The first thing I said was, "I'm in recovery. I don't do that anymore."

He said, "Good for you. Here's my number if you ever need me."

I said, "I don't think so." And he left. I was so proud of myself. That's when I knew I was getting really strong.

JOYCE: Jamie asked me to be her birth coach and I was thrilled to accept that honor. The birthing room was filled with our friends. As Hannah was born, we all sang the song we had written for her birth. My heart was so full of gratitude and love for Jamie, love for this beautiful new baby and for life itself.

JAMIE: When it was all over and my parents left, I started to panic. What was I going to do with this baby? One of the nurses came in and we started to talk. I told her I was in recovery and talked about my story. At the end of it, she asked if I was in pain and offered me Demerol. I couldn't believe it. I had just finished telling her I was an addict. She was a nice enough person, but she didn't link the two things together. Don't give an addict drugs, legal or not!

———◆———

In the first few years of recovery, I did think about using or having a drink. In my early recovery, I craved narcotics intensely every day. Today I don't have the same intense craving for alcohol or drugs.

Sometimes, though, I think I crave the not feeling, the numbness that you get when you're high. I didn't like having to feel. I didn't like feeling disappointment or sadness or hurt. I'm not used to dealing with feelings, because of all those years that I didn't feel at all. Experiencing real feelings is new to me. Today, I'm grateful for all my feelings—both the pain and the joy. In the first few years of my recovery, if I felt stressed or emotional, and I hadn't gone to a meeting, that's when I would start thinking about alcohol or drugs. And for one split second I would think, "Maybe I should stop and get some. Well, god, it will make me feel better; why not?" No thinking about the consequences. But I'd go to a meeting and be reminded to play the tape all the way through to the end.

Now my disease manifests itself in other ways in my life. I still can get obsessed with a thought or a worry. I often act compulsively. Using is a symptom of our disease. Once I put the drugs down, I had to deal with all the reasons I had used them to begin with. I have learned to use the tools the 12-step program has given me. I attend meetings on a regular basis; I continue to work the 12-step program. I keep in close contact with my sponsor and the women I sponsor.

This gives me the support to walk in gratitude, knowing I have everything I need.

I'm often asked, "What made you stop? When did enough become enough?" The answer to this question may be different for other recovering addicts. There were so many nights when I would be on my hands and knees praying to stop using. Near the end, death became a better option than quitting. I felt as though I had nothing to live for, regardless of the love around me. I had almost surrendered and considered myself hopeless. I was deemed to use for the rest of my life. I felt The Beast had won.

But the answer to the question of why I stopped is that I began to know that I had to want to live just a little bit more than I wanted to die. And in wanting to live, I had to choose not wanting to use, because for me, to use was to die. So I had to think and say, "I don't want to use." At first, I could get through only an hour; it wasn't a day at a time—it was an hour at a time. I started to feel that something inside me was fighting The Beast and I realized I wasn't alone anymore. I had another life to fight for. I told myself that even if I wasn't worth it, another life was. So I mustered the little bit of strength I had to let myself feel this. As I let the thought sink in, I found the courage to face The Beast and recognize it as my abductor. With all the will I had, I fought The Beast, one hour at a time, then one day at a time. It took a long time before I began to understand that I was getting strong because I had chosen the light over the darkness The Beast cast upon me. The more I began to like who I was, the more I could accept being liked. The Beast wouldn't allow me to feel the love that was always around me. Now through clean and sober eyes, I could see it had always kept me from knowing the truth. The truth was, I was worthy. Knowing that, I chose life.

I began to lay the foundation for my recovery and my new life, just as Carol Anne's family did at the end of *Poltergeist*.

Some Final Thoughts

O UR HOPE IN writing this book is to share the daily thoughts, conversations, struggles and successes in the process of addiction and recovery, with particular emphasis on the impact it has on the addicted person, the family and the extended community. The past seven years haven't been easy. They have, however, been rewarding. Recovery is a continuous process—there is no end to it. That is why there really can be no end to this book, just a closing chapter to this part of the journey.

Jamie's daughter is now six years old. Jamie celebrated seven years of recovery last fall. She works hard at sobriety, continues to go to meetings and has daily contact with her sponsor. She knew prior to active addiction that she wanted a career in helping people. It was only by getting clean that she was able to achieve that dream. She has held various positions in the human-services field in the seven years she has been clean. She is currently working on her CASAC (Credentialed Alcohol and Substance Abuse Counselor) certificate and is contemplating going back for her master's degree. The most important thing is that she has hope and focuses each day on living.

The body of forgiveness work that John has created over the past 30 years has touched the lives of many people. He still sees individual clients, leads groups in A Course in Miracles and conducts Webinars on forgiveness. He has begun work on a book about the sweetness of forgiveness.

Joyce, through her company Vision Power, leads people and organizations in a process of creating powerful new possibilities in their lives.

Addiction takes a tremendous toll on the lives it touches. We are eternally grateful for all the people in the rooms who prayed for Jamie and us when she didn't even consider going to meetings. We are so appreciative of each agency along the way that contributed to her recovery. Denise, the sponsor of sponsors, will always hold a special place in our hearts. We are grateful for the friends of Jamie who had the courage to stand up to her and sometimes leave her until she entered recovery. We still grieve for the friends she made in recovery whose lives were taken in early sobriety. We are especially thankful for those on the other side who were cheering us on during the most perilous times of our lives. Last, we are deeply grateful to our spiritual community, our friends and family and the many angels who appeared along the way to help us make the right turn when the road was so dark.

We hope that by sharing our very personal story, families who read it can take action when action is indicated. Although we did not attend Al-Anon, we know that this is a phenomenal program that has helped millions of people. We strongly encourage those who are affected by alcohol or other substances to attend this life-changing program. We hope that our story lends courage to stand for recovery. We hope it brings understanding of the power of forgiveness. It is only in the present moment that we have the power to release the chains of the past. If you will forgive the things not said or done, and the things in your own unhealed past that led to missteps in the present, you can be lifted from the shame that addiction carries. Through new eyes, you can create a new future that is unencumbered by unexamined beliefs. That future holds the possibility of experiencing unconditional love, the most powerful force on earth.

This recovery process has taught each member of our family valuable lessons. Through it all, even in our mistakes, we stood for life. We remain standing for life—for ourselves, for those who came before us and will come after us. We hope you are inspired to stand for life in your own continuing story.

Acknowledgments

THIS BOOK COULD not have been written without the help of some very special people. The first is our friend Lisa, who believed that the message we had to relay was so important that she volunteered to coach us through the writing of the book. During the drafts, she sat with us and transcribed our story, all the while encouraging us to continue. Her belief in the importance of this book, her courage and her insights helped us reach the point where we can now say "We're glad we did it."

When Lisa could no longer continue as our coach, we were forced to decide whether or not it made sense to continue. We had the audacity to ask friends—those who had expertise in the field of addiction, had children who were in recovery or were still using, or those who had lived with us through the events portrayed—to read the draft and offer suggestions for improvement. We are most grateful to Sue, Darlene, Diane, Linda, Cherie, Jessica, Denise, Ellen and John for their honesty and thoughtful feedback, which inspired us to dedicate our energy to the completion of this book.

It was clear from their feedback that we needed an editor to give us the tools to reach our destination. Arlene moved to our small city with a lifetime of extraordinary credentials as a copy editor. We summoned the courage to ask her to read our rough manuscript and to critique it. We asked her to tell us the truth. Did she think this was a good book or were we deluding ourselves? Was it worth spending another year of our time, emotional commitment and financial investment to involve her as an editor? Within a day she asked for a meeting. It was clear from the moment we met that Arlene would be the driving force to see this project to its completion. It was her expertise, her command of the language and her loving process of "inquiry" that motivated us to complete this book. Her belief in us, and our message, and her love of the written word created an environment in which the yearlong process of revision produced this book as well as an enduring friendship.

ABOUT THE AUTHORS

· · · · · · · ·

JOHN CHUPKA is the founder of The Forgiveness Center, a spiritually based practice of psychotherapy and transpersonal education in Troy, New York. A psychotherapist in private practice for 35 years, he has also produced CDs of healing meditations, *Transcending for Men* and *Transcending for Women*, which have had dramatic results. John received his MSW from Syracuse University and is a licensed clinical social worker. He has been trained in brief strategic therapy and Ericksonian hypnosis. He is also a creative humorist and a singer-songwriter.

JOYCE QUARANTA CHUPKA coaches CEOs, executive teams and individuals to create and implement inspirational strategic plans. She left her 30-year career as an executive-level public administrator, government lobbyist and community leader to write and to design a unique value-based vision process to assist her clients. Joyce holds an MPA from the Kennedy School of Government at Harvard University. Both she and John are honored to be members of the Transformational Leadership Council.

In the seven years of her sobriety, **JAMIE CHUPKA** has graduated from college with a bachelor's degree in science, raised her daughter, worked as a clinician and as an HIV Prevention Educator. She hopes to return to college for her master's degree while simultaneously working toward her CASAC (Credentialed Alcohol and Substance Abuse Counselor). Jamie continues to raise her beautiful, spirited, energetic daughter and is learning about self-worth, self-love and forgiveness.